Bhagawan Nityananda
of
Ganeshpuri

BHAGAWAN NITYANANDA
of
GANESHPURI

by
SWAMI MUKTANANDA
PARAMAHAMSA

A SIDDHA YOGA PUBLICATION
PUBLISHED BY SYDA FOUNDATION

Published by SYDA Foundation
371 Brickman Rd., South Fallsburg, New York 12779-0600, USA

ACKNOWLEDGMENTS

Grateful appreciation goes to Smita Shroff and Garima Borwankar for their translation of Part One from the original Hindi; to Hemananda and to George Reading for their editorial assistance; to Shane Conroy for his cover illustration; to Hans Turstig for transliteration from the Devanagari; to Dada Yande, Swami Shantananda, Swami Kripananda, Marilyn Goldin, Arthur Novell, Stratford Sherman, and Peggy Bendet for reviewing the text; to Diane Fast for copyediting the text and for compiling the glossary; to Cheryl Crawford for cover and text design; to Stéphane Dehais for typesetting; and to Osnat Shurer, Sushila Traverse, and Valerie Sensabaugh for overseeing the production of this book.

Sarah Scott
Editor

Cover illustration:
Bhagawan Nityananda, from a photograph taken September 24, 1926

Part One is a new translation from the original Hindi, published as *Bhagawan Nityananda, Jivan Aur Karya* in 1968, and first published in English as *Bhagawan Nityananda* in 1972 by Gurudev Siddha Peeth, Ganeshpuri, India.

Printed in the United States of America

Library of Congress Cataloging-in-Publication Data

Muktananda, Swami, 1908—
    Bhagawan Nityananda of Ganeshpuri / by Swami Muktananda Paramahamsa.
        p.   cm.
    "A Siddha Yoga publication."
    ISBN 0-911307-45-1 (pbk.)
    1. Nityananda, Swami, 1897-1961.   2. Hindus—India—Biography.
    I. Title.
    BL1175.N48M85 1996
    294.5'513'092—dc20   96-3550
    [B]   CIP

Contents

A NOTE ON THE TEXT

For simplicity, Sanskrit and Hindi words such as *darshan* and *sadhana*, which are commonly used in Siddha Yoga courses and publications, are printed in the text in roman type. Less familiar words appear in italic. The long vowels in italicized Sanskrit words are indicated in the text with a bar above the letter. For the interested student, all Sanskrit words in the Glossary are also presented according to the conventions of the international style of transliteration.

FOREWORD

*R*ain poured down in sheets. In the enclosed veranda, the atmosphere was filled with sulphurous odors from the nearby hot springs. A few rain-drenched visitors were staring, wide-eyed, through the bars of a window at the ebony figure seated alone on a hard wooden bench inside. He was as motionless as a black granite statue — gazing into space far beyond human vision.

The visitors waited expectantly for some indication that this being was alive and not merely a statue. But he seemed totally unaware of their presence. Then, after a few minutes, the figure did move: he lowered his gaze and spoke. A high-pitched voice broke the silence of the dark, rainy afternoon. He spoke in a strange language, addressing no one in particular, and continued speaking until everyone present felt as if he were speaking to him or her alone.

My rain-soaked clothes were completely dry by now and I started sweating under them when he looked at me and asked, "Did you take a bath in the hot springs? Did you have darshan of Vajreshwari?" Awestruck, I could only nod.

This was my first meeting with Bhagawan Nityananda in Ganeshpuri, forty-three years ago.

Bhagawan Nityananda was a giant among the Siddha Masters of his time. There have been very few who have equaled his stature throughout history. Nevertheless, his life was

Swami Muktananda

completely shrouded in mystery until Swami Muktananda, his worthy disciple and heir, opened the treasure-house of his own spiritual experiences to thousands of seekers. I am one of those, for it was only when Nityananda sent me to Muktananda in June of 1961 that I was shown who Nityananda truly was and is.

Baba Muktananda wrote and spoke often about Bhagawan Nityananda, extolling the primordial greatness of his Guru. Previously, we had heard only about Nityananda's supernatural powers and miracles, and these did have their own intrinsic value for some people. Nevertheless, such stories tended to focus attention on things such as material well-being. Swami Muktananda shifted this emphasis to the immense spiritual wealth hidden in the unfathomable depths of his Guru. He pointed out that the greatest miracle is inner transformation and the ever-increasing knowledge of the Self — that divinity existing within all. He taught that the key to this transformation is meditation, and the secret of meditation is the awakening of the Kundalini energy by a Siddha Guru.

Bhagawan Nityananda frequently said that to understand a Siddha, one must become a Siddha. The unique feature of this book is that it contains the words of a being who has become one with his Guru. Since Baba Muktananda himself is a perfect Siddha Master, this book is a perfect description of Nityananda's life and teachings. To understand these teachings in their fullness, however, one must dive deeply within one's own being, guided by the grace of the Siddha Masters. And the more we hear about these Masters, the more easily we are able to dive deeply within ourselves. The outer form of the Master has changed: Just as Bhagawan Nityananda passed on to Swami Muktananda the full power of the Siddha Yoga lineage, so Muktananda passed this same attainment and power on to Gurumayi Chidvilasananda. The formless inner Shakti, the primordial universal Consciousness, continues to shine through her in all its effulgence, bringing inner unfoldment and right understanding to earnest seekers throughout the world.

Bhagawan Nityananda of Ganeshpuri is an introduction to this eternal mystery and play of Consciousness. It is an aid to seekers who want to experience the essence of the teachings of Siddha

Swami Chidvilasananda

Yoga: to realize their own divinity and to see God in one another. "Bow to your own Self, respect your Self, worship your own Self, because God dwells within you as you, for you." This is the divine message of Swami Muktananda, born of his own Self-realization. This book lovingly reveals — for Baba loved his Guru more than life itself — the source of Baba's divine inner state and understanding, his beloved Bhagawan Nityananda.

— Shree Pratap N. "Dada" Yande
January 15, 1996
Ganeshpuri, India

Shree Pratap N. Yande *was brought up in a family that worshiped saints and Siddhas. When he was twenty, he met the great Siddha Shree Gajanan Maharaj of Nasik, who predicted a career in government administration for him. This marked the start of a long, successful career in the government of Maharashtra. It was in 1953 that Shree Yande first visited Ganeshpuri, but not until his second visit in 1961 did he become aware of Bhagawan Nityananda's greatness. It was also at this time that Bhagawan sent him to Swami Muktananda, who affectionately began to address him as "Dada" (elder brother). Dada served Baba Muktananda in many ways over the next two decades, with selfless service ranging from helping to administer Gurudev Siddha Peeth — the ashram that Bhagawan commanded Baba to found — to taking dictation for part of Baba's landmark spiritual autobiography,* Play of Consciousness. *Since Baba's mahāsamādhi in 1982, Dada has been serving Gurumayi Chidvilasananda with the same devotion and commitment — most recently, performing the service of translating Gurumayi's books into Marathi.*

PREFACE

*B*hagawan *Nityananda of Ganeshpuri* is a modern story of devotion in an ancient lineage of discipleship. Coming fourteen years after Swami Muktananda's passing, these are his words, his thoughts, his offering of praise to his Guru, compiled from many sources, across many years.

This book is comprised of three sections. Part One is Baba Muktananda's written portrait, reflective and contemplative. The scope widens in Part Two to tell the story of his interactions with his Guru during his years of spiritual practice. In Part Three, the book expands even further as Muktananda invites us all to join in the joyous legacy of discipleship.

Part One is the biography that Swami Muktananda first published in Hindi in 1968, and then in English as *Bhagawan Nityananda* in 1972. This is a new rendering, based on a fresh translation that returns to both the structure and the content of the Hindi edition. The writing in Part One is formal and elevated, a tribute to Bhagawan's life and work. So steady is the focus that the author himself is almost invisible, his personality submerged in his devotion and reverence. One can imagine Baba in the small ashram that Gurudev Siddha Peeth was in 1968, writing this portrait, capturing his memories on the page.

In the final chapter of Part One, Baba writes: "Shree Gurudev's influence and presence were, in themselves, so powerful that he did not need to give lectures or teach explicitly. Even so, the devotees always hoped for a few words from him; they were eager to know how he would answer their questions. For their sake, Gurudev would occasionally speak a little."

What his Guru presented in such condensed form, Baba expands and illuminates with personal experiences and anecdotes in Parts Two and Three. With compassion he fulfills the desires of devotees who asked him: How did you meet your Guru? What was your spiritual practice like? Was it long? Was it difficult? How do his teachings relate to our lives?

These and other such questions Baba answered as he traveled the world between 1970 and 1982, sharing the teachings and practices of Siddha Yoga Meditation with thousands of seekers. Parts Two and Three are edited from his talks and writings during that period. The material is therefore woven together from many sources: an anecdote at a public program in Australia, an answer to a question in New York, a contemplation written in the silence of his study. Parts of the material were retrieved from transcripts of Swami Muktananda's talks and are only now being published. Some of it has appeared in other Siddha Yoga publications. All of it is collected together here for the first time.

Bhagawan Nityananda of Ganeshpuri presents a full picture, a close view of a spiritual Master through the clear eyes of one who became a Master himself. It is an intimate look at a relationship that led to liberation for the disciple — and to the promise of liberation for all those who pursue this path. And as Baba said: "This lineage will never be broken. Baba Nityananda, my Guru, gave me his work to do. Similarly, when I leave this world, I will have to make someone else responsible for this work." Before Baba Muktananda passed away in 1982, he kept his promise by transmitting the power and authority of the lineage of Siddha Yoga Masters to Gurumayi Chidvilasananda, just as Bhagawan Nityananda had empowered him more than twenty years earlier. It was Gurumayi who envisioned this book, and it is through her grace that it became a reality. In relating to Gurumayi, the living Master of Siddha Yoga, we are inextricably linked to Baba Muktananda and through him, to Bhagawan Nityananda. As Baba declared: "You are all the Nityananda family."

— *Sarah Scott, Editor*
Monterey, California
February 8, 1996

INTRODUCTION

$\mathcal{T}$housands of people came for the darshan of Bhagawan Nityananda, and most of them came for relief from their personal difficulties. This was not why I came. I came because I wanted some kind of glimpse of the inner wisdom — *jñāna*. There was a group of six or seven of us — justices, lawyers, a university vice-chancellor — who would come to receive Bhagawan's wisdom. He would speak in monosyllables, but his words manifested the experience of Self-realization. It was because he was established in the state of divine Consciousness all the time that he could touch and thrill the hearts of the people who came before him for his darshan.

Around that same time, I happened to meet a *sannyāsi* in Gavdevi village on my way back from having Bhagawan's darshan in Ganeshpuri. The *sannyāsi* came out of his room, smiling softly as he looked at me, and then he started talking in a very informal and relaxed manner. Although he was unassuming in his talk, I was struck by his keen intelligence and all-encompassing understanding. He had a razor-sharp intellect and was able to make me understand, in very simple words, how a person can achieve unity with God's creation as long as there is purity of heart. That *sannyāsi* was Swami Muktananda.

Whatever words were uttered by Bhagawan Nityananda, I would write them down and place them at the feet of Baba Muktananda. Then Baba would give a lecture. Sometimes he would speak for an hour on each sentence. Many people used to gather to hear Swami Muktananda because of his commentaries on the words that Bhagawan had spoken.

For a short while I was in active political life, although not as a politician. I was representing the cause of some small holders in Maharashtra, and I thought that some injustice had been done to them, so I decided to fast. I first went to Swami Muktananda, however, and when he heard my story he said: "Look, Parulekar, this is a very complicated matter. You had better go and see the 'Supreme Court.'" That was Bhagawan Nityananda! Bhagawan listened and then he told me to do it, but to do it in a diplomatic manner. So I came back with a happy heart. I met Baba and told him what Bhagawan had said. Quietly, Baba Muktananda took an apple and gave it to me. He said, "Before you start your fast, please eat it." I ate that fruit and for three days felt such inner expansion that I ate nothing else. After those three days, the purpose of the fast was served.

Bhagawan did not always encourage us to rely on him for our decisions. At one time I was offered a position as a member judge of the Revenue Tribunal, and my wife's father suggested that I ask Bhagawan if I should accept the position. To please him I came, but Bhagawan got angry and said: "Why do you come here for every small thing? God has given you the intellect; you decide for yourself."

Undoubtedly, one of the greatest gifts that I received from Bhagawan Nityananda was the ability to focus my mind. He would just look at me and my thoughts would settle, and because of such concentration of mind all went well and I was able to achieve what I have achieved in my life. In fact, on the very first occasion that I met him, Bhagawan uttered three phrases that continue to have profound meaning for me. He said, "*Nirmala mana; nishchala mana; vishāla mana.*" (Purified mind; unwavering mind; immutable mind that is vast, that is eternal.) Now, whenever my mind is afflicted with doubts or worries over mundane matters, I think of these precious words — words that contain the essence and fullness of Indian spirituality — to help bring my mind back to its true abode.

It was Swami Muktananda who gave me the understanding of

that and many other significant and divine utterances. Baba was a very great soul. He could talk to a child or to a scholar, each on their own level. Very few people had access to Bhagawan's teachings — it was my good fortune that I had the chance to sit at his feet — but Baba Muktananda used to explain these teachings in such a way that all could understand.

It is therefore very appropriate that Swami Muktananda should write the biography of his revered Guru. Who else but he could understand the full meaning of Bhagawan's profound teachings? Who else but he could unravel their mystery for devotees of every background? And through this book of Baba's, Bhagawan Nityananda — the great *avadhūt* of Ganeshpuri — continues to bless and enrich the lives of those who read about him.

— *Shree D.M. Parulekar*
February 5, 1996
Bombay, India

Shree D.M. Parulekar *met Bhagawan Nityananda in 1950. Together with a small group of fellow seekers, he was privileged to sit at Bhagawan's feet and to hear his sutra-like teachings. He collected these words and took them to Baba Muktananda after each session so that Baba would elucidate their meaning. Then, in 1961, Shree Parulekar published this record under the title Tuza Visara Nawhawa ("Do Not Let Me Forget You"). A lawyer by profession, Shree Parulekar has become a recognized and highly respected authority on the laws relating to land tenure. He is a frequent contributor to a number of prestigious law journals and newspapers, and has published several books relating to his field of expertise.*

Bhagawan Nityananda
of
Ganeshpuri

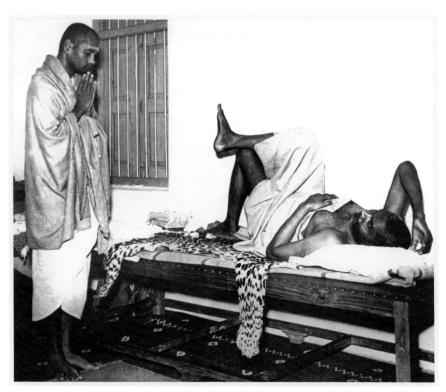

Swami Muktananda with his Guru, Bhagawan Nityananda

Invocation

O Gurudev, you are my Self, supreme bliss.
Through your inspiration, I have written this.
You alone will read it,
you who live within everyone
and are experienced as the Self.
O compassionate and merciful one!
Even union with the Absolute is petty
compared to the extraordinary experience
of your inner love.
From you alone, one attains interest in attaining
the bliss of the Self.
You are all, and all are you.
Om Guru, Jaya Guru.
O Shree Guru, I hail you.

Sadgurunath Maharaj ki Jay!

PART ONE

Bhagawan Nityananda

CHAPTER ONE

From Time to Time the Lord Takes Birth

What is this world, this universe? What is the essence of this cosmos? Some say the world is a wheel of birth and death, that we live and die and are then reborn. Some say this world is real; others unreal. Some say it exists and others that it does not. Some say it is both real and unreal, both existent and non-existent. There are many different explanations of the world.

Whatever this world may be, one thing is certain: it is full of wonder. However puzzling it may be, there is no doubt that its Creator has made it with great skill and artistry.

A thoughtful person muses from time to time: if there were no sun, where would we find light and heat? If there were no moon, where would we find coolness? If the air didn't move, how would we live? Without water, how would our thirst be quenched? And if the earth didn't grow vegetables and grains, fruits and medicinal plants, what would we eat?

If there were no green trees and leaves, no fruits and flowers, no majestic mountains and flowing rivers, nature would not be so beautiful. And if there were no animals or birds, the wilderness would not be so beautiful, fierce, and grand. This amazing diversity exists among people as well.

All this variety enables the world to function. Every thing and every person plays its part. Just as all these elements are necessary for the world, even more necessary are meditation and spirituality. They are essential. This is why, time after time, saints and great beings come to this world. They take birth in order to uplift humanity. Their lifestyle may seem strange and puzzling, but many kinds of people — depressed, poor, sad, desperate, homeless — find peace, contentment, and an inner satisfaction in their presence. For this reason the compassionate Lord takes the form of saints and great beings, and appears in this world from time to time.

And so it was that an extraordinary being came to live in Ganeshpuri to fulfill a divine mission. He came to be known by his devotees as Bhagawan Nityananda.

His Birth

No one knows where my beloved Gurudev was born, where he grew up, and where he did his sadhana, his spiritual practice. None of this history has been preserved. Even though no one has any definite knowledge about his family, in reality it is no more important to know the ancestry of saints and great beings than it is to find the source of the Ganges and other holy rivers. As with rivers, so with saints — it is their influence, the extraordinary effect of their grace that really matters.

In the *Shrīmad Bhāgavatam* it is said:

na yasya janma-karmabhyam no varnasrama-jatibhih /
sajjate asmin-aham-bhavo dehe vai sa hareh priyah // [11.2:51]

This means: "One who is not attached to his body, one who is not proud about his birth, his actions, or his social status — such a being is dear to the Lord."

My Gurudev was such a being. Beyond the shadow of a doubt, he was a born Siddha. Even when he was a child, he possessed astonishing *siddhis*, amazing divine powers. These *siddhis* did not even require his physical presence. To this very day his Samadhi Shrine is pervaded by these divine powers, and countless pure seekers are blessed beyond measure by them.

Lost in supreme bliss, his face was always illuminated with a radiant, sweet, and compassionate smile. From time to time, he would laugh, and that laughter still echoes in my memory. Because he loved to smile, people came to address him as Nityananda, one who is always in bliss. In the end this was the name by which he was famous.

Ever since he was a young man, his head was clean-shaven. Before coming to Vajreshwari he sometimes wore the saffron robes of a monk, so perhaps he had been initiated into the Nandapadma Order.

GURUVAN
AND SURROUNDINGS

It seems that Shree Gurudev appeared as a young man, some fifty or sixty years ago, in South Karnataka, at a place called Guruvan, near Kanhangad. He sometimes described the place. It was hilly and densely wooded. In the forest were wild animals, snakes, and poisonous plants. In the hills was a very deep cave, and for a long time my Guru lived in this cave in a state of deep meditation.

The place is known as his *tapobhūmi*, or site of spiritual practice, and that is why it was named Guruvan, which means the Guru's forest. It is regarded as a place where *siddhis*, or psychic powers, can be attained. Nearby are eight huge stones, symbols of the eight psychic powers.

Since there was no water supply nearby, my Guru created a stream within the cave, and it has been flowing ever since. This holy stream is called Papnashini Ganga, and the name suggests that drinking from the stream, or bathing in it, will wash away impurities.

Shree Gurudev was very fond of gardens, and he planted coconut palms, mangos, jackfruit, and betelnut trees there. The trees he planted and the stream he made are still there, and they can be seen today. The beauty and peace of this place make it very appropriate for *tapasya*, austerities.

Even today, hundreds of devotees come to have the darshan

of this sacred place, whose every particle is permeated by the power of Shree Gurudev's austerities. People from Mangalore regard Guruvan as a sacred place of pilgrimage, and on the occasion of Bhagawan's *punyātithi*, the anniversary of the day he left his body, they go there to chant, to offer worship, and to have their hearts' desires fulfilled.

Three or four miles from Guruvan, Shree Gurudev established a large ashram. About a mile from the beach, at the edge of the village of Kanhangad, the ashram lies in the midst of lush green fields and groves of coconut palms. In the distance are mountains spreading as far as the eye can see. The beauty of the place makes the mind feel happy.

At one time the fort of Hosdurg stood here. Nearby is a cliff with many caves where the soldiers used to hide. Gurudev transformed them from soldiers' caves to meditation caves, and now there are more than forty of them. This is where Bhagawan would sit when devotees came for his darshan. Even now, people who meditate in these caves experience the divine Shakti, and some even experience the state of samadhi, union with God.

The ashram is fairly good-sized, with many large rooms. A mile away, near the beach, is a place called Khusalnagar, where Gurudev lived for some time. The area is surrounded by coconut trees and is extremely beautiful. Gurudev had a well constructed there for the benefit of the local people.

HIS EARLY TRAVELS AND LILAS

*I*t was in Kerala and Mangalore in South India where Bhagawan Nityananda enacted many of his *līlās*, or divine plays, and performed many miracles. He traveled on foot, roaming freely in Dharmasthala, Kapu, Mulki, Udipi, Padubidri, Kanhangad, Kasargod, Bantwal, Gokarna, and various other places. During his travels he freed many people from illness, sorrow, pain, and poverty. Even today the people of that area remember him with tears of gratitude, and sometimes they come to Ganeshpuri to have the darshan of his Samadhi Shrine.

Shree Gurudev loved solitude, and he lived alone. He usually traveled on foot, moving through the woods and mountains with lightning speed. People say he could move from one place to another at the speed of thought. He never stayed anywhere for long. He would travel from one village to another in a state of total bliss; for him, divine joy existed everywhere. He accepted food and water only if they were offered to him, since he never felt their want. He lived in a state of childlike innocence.

There are many stories of miracles from this period. As the accounts of his miraculous powers were told, more and more people followed him. To avoid the crowds, he kept on the move. Sometimes he even climbed trees and from there he would casually toss down leaves as medicine to people who were sick. Devotees would accept the gift and become well again. Sometimes his mere presence would heal people.

Stories are told of other kinds of miracles too. He built many caves and rest houses without taking money from anyone. He would tell the workers to take their wages from under any stone in the jungle, and they used to get the right amount. Or he would put his hand in his loincloth and take out the right amount without even counting.

When the ashram was being built in Kanhangad, the police came to investigate. They wanted to know where Gurudev was getting the money. He led the police through the wild jungle to a lake full of crocodiles, jumped into the water, and pulled out bundle after bundle of brand-new rupee notes, which he tossed to the police. Frightened and astonished, the police bowed to him and ran away.

One day a government official put Gurudev in jail, thinking he was some crazy vagrant. But when Bhagawan was seen on the road outside the jail — at the same time that he was seen inside the jail — the official realized he was dealing with a great being, and he released him immediately.

Occasionally Gurudev would get on a train. If he was asked for a ticket, he would produce thousands of tickets from his loincloth. If he was asked to get off, the train would stop and not run anymore.

Local people saw him walking on the waters of the Pavanja

River. Many times he fed thousands of people with sweets, and no one had the slightest idea where the sweets came from.

Shree Gurudev was the object of envy and jealousy from people who did not understand his state. They thought he was stupid and crazy, and they used to abuse him, not only insulting him with words but even throwing things at his bare body: lumps of clay, cow dung, and stones. He was never the least bit bothered by this.

Once a malicious man named Apayya, who knew some black magic, offered Gurudev poisoned tobacco. Gurudev swallowed it. Nothing happened to him, but Apayya began to writhe in agony from the pain in his stomach, and he soon died.

Similarly, someone from Malbar in South India caught hold of Gurudev, tied up his hands with rags soaked in kerosene, and set him on fire. But it was the Malbari who died in agony from the flames. Gurudev was untouched.

On one of his travels through various villages, my Gurudev came to a village named Bantwal on the bank of the Netravati River. Here again, ignorant people harassed him as they had done elsewhere. Suddenly, Shree Gurudev disappeared and went into the jungle, where he could be in solitude, far away from the duplicity and scheming of the people.

Then a remarkable thing happened. It was as if the Netravati River herself could no longer bear the insults given to a great being like Gurudev Nityananda, and she decided to punish the foolish villagers. The river in her fury took on the fierce aspect of the Lord. Unexpectedly, the Netravati rose and began to flood the village. Many houses and people and animals were in danger, and some were carried away by the flood waters. The frightened villagers ran helter-skelter to save their lives.

With danger so near, they remembered God and dharma. They also remembered Shree Gurudev. The wiser ones saw the connection between his disappearance and the flood. They searched for him but could not find him. In fear they prayed to him. Feeling compassion for the suffering people, Gurudev appeared on the opposite bank of the swollen river. At the sight of him, the river became calm, and gradually the waters subsided.

Many such stories are heard about Shree Gurudev.

HIS DIVINE POWERS

*H*ere we should remember that Gurudev never consciously performed any miracles himself. He was completely absorbed in God, in cosmic Consciousness. He saw the same divine Truth in himself and in everything else. For him there was no essential difference between a dog, a cat, a priest, and a king. In his eyes all were made of the same essence, just as in the eyes of a goldsmith all the ornaments, whatever their size and shape, are made of gold and nothing else. Shree Gurudev had no sense of separation, of individuality; he had become one with supreme Consciousness. Therefore, supernatural powers waited on him reverently, and as a result, miracles large and small took place spontaneously.

These divine powers were nothing like the tricks that some people learn to do by practicing austerities. Such people can move their hand in a circle and manifest some *kumkum*, or a piece of fruit, or a gold necklace. *Siddhis* like these depend on the type of austerity practiced, and they last only a short time.

It was entirely different with my Gurudev. The eight divine powers stood in attendance on him, just as we stand ready to serve a great being for our upliftment and liberation. Without Gurudev doing anything, these powers would do their work.

The all-pervading Shakti, the divine energy, was fully developed in Shree Gurudev, and all kinds of miracles happened through him. Superficial *siddhis* acquired by artificial means are worthless, but those that come of their own accord to a great being are beneficial. This was certainly true in the case of my Gurudev. Everything was possible for him.

The sages have spoken about three types of *siddhis*. There are impure powers acquired through unclean vows and incantations. After the practitioner bathes and becomes clean, he can no longer perform them. This kind of power has only evil effects; there is nothing good about it.

Then there are mantra *siddhis*, acquired by saying a mantra to a particular deity under certain conditions. This kind of power allows you to manifest a piece of fruit or an ornament in your hand, or move an object from one place to another. Such miracles impress and attract people for a time, but this kind of magic does not last long.

Then there are the true *siddhis*, those described in the scriptures. These powers are acquired by practicing with rigorous discipline the eight steps of *ashtānga yoga*. These steps require virtuous behavior, physical discipline, the ability to restrain the senses from their outward pull, concentration, and deep meditation that reaches the state of unity-consciousness. Far beyond these three *siddhis*, however, is a supreme power, the *mahāsiddhi*. This is not acquired by one's own efforts. It is a gift from God, and it always brings His presence. It is, in fact, the divine power of God Himself. Just as a drop of rain which falls into the ocean becomes indistinguishable from the ocean, in the same way, one who has merged with God becomes indistinguishable from God. Near such a being dwells this *mahāsiddhi*, waiting with folded hands and always ready to do his work.

In the *Shiva Sūtras*, it is said:

shuddhavidyodayācchakreshatva-siddhih / [1.21]

When pure knowledge arises, one attains mastery over all the divine powers.

Such powers do not require that one perform austerities, do *japa*, engage in rituals, or make vows. A great soul who has such powers does not even realize that he has them. They manifest of their own accord and perform their service for his devotees. This is the reason why so many miracles and otherwise inexplicable events happened around my Gurudev.

CHAPTER TWO

Ganeshpuri: Land of Yoga

Ganeshpuri is the sacred land of yoga,
where the worthy king of yogis abides.
By remembrance of him, supreme bliss is obtained.
I bow to you, O venerable Nityananda!

After several years in south India, Shree Gurudev set out on
a pilgrimage. He covered the whole of India, blessing it with his
lotus feet. He must have visited every corner of the country
because he used to describe each pilgrimage site in great detail,
saying that he had been there.

There is a story that Gurudev performed intense austerities in
the Himalayas, living for six years in the top of a tree. Bhagawan
Nityananda was a supreme soul, ecstatic and fully conscious, and
for such a divine soul, everything is quite possible. But it is a fact
that Gurudev was a born Siddha, and he had no need for austerities. Even so, to be a living example, to encourage seekers, he
sometimes did perform austerities.

After traveling the length and breadth of India, Shree Gurudev
came to a famous holy place in western India in the state of

Maharashtra.* It is called Vajreshwari. High on a rock stands an ancient temple, so large that it can be seen from a great distance. It is a *devī* temple, dedicated to the Goddess Vajreshwari. It was built by Shree Chimnaji Appa, a Maratha ruler, who won a battle against the Portuguese at Vasai with the grace of the goddess. Five of the surrounding villages were assigned to the temple to ensure its proper maintenance.

For the benefit of the local people, Shree Gurudev built two rest houses for travelers, a restaurant, a well, a clinic, a maternity home, and a high school.

Near Vajreshwari is a village called Akloli, where there are sacred hot springs called Ramkunda. Here Gurudev built another rest house for travelers and a deep well. He also renovated the hot springs by the river.

During his early days in Maharashtra, Shree Gurudev was often seen in Akloli and Vajreshwari. Later on, after appeals from devotees, he settled permanently in Ganeshpuri, a mile and a half from Vajreshwari, near the hot springs of the Bhimeshwar Mahadev Temple. Here he spent the last twenty-five to thirty years of his life on this earth.

What was it about the ancient land of Ganeshpuri that appealed so much to Shree Gurudev?

Just as Lord Vishnu settled in Vaikuntha and Lord Shiva in Kailas, Shree Gurudev settled in the sacred land of Ganeshpuri. It is an ancient and holy place. Overlooking the valley is Mount Mandagni, where Siddhas have performed austerities. The river Tejasa, lovely and purifying, flows through the valley. There are dense jungles, rich with flowers and fruits. There are famous hot springs. And there is the venerable temple of the *devī* in Vajreshwari. Ages ago, the sage Vasishtha performed a large *yajña* here, a fire ceremony. At that time, according to tradition, Vasishtha installed an image of Lord Ganesh in a temple — and that is how this land came to be known as Ganeshpuri.

And so this spiritually-charged landscape, once a wish-fulfilling place for devotees of long ago, was brought to life again by Gurudev. He came and stayed and made it immortal. Shree

---

*Although the date has not been historically established, some eyewitnesses say he arrived in the Tansa Valley around 1936.

Gurudev changed the look of Ganeshpuri completely. Once deserted, it has become a paradise.

Wherever saints live, people are drawn there and settlements spring up quite naturally. The village of Shirdi grew up around Sai Baba, and Ganeshpuri grew up around Bhagawan Nityananda.

FROM WILDERNESS TO THRIVING VILLAGE

*B*efore Shree Gurudev came to Ganeshpuri, it was a wilderness full of wild animals. Except for an ancient Shiva temple and some hot springs beside it — both overgrown with vegetation — there was not a single building. But after Gurudev came to live there, in a simple hut near the hot springs, the empty wilderness was gradually transformed into a village full of people.

The first thing Shree Gurudev did was to renovate the temple and the hot springs. In this ancient temple is a *shivalingam* known as Bhimeshwar Mahadev. A continuous trickle of holy water seeps from inside the dome of the temple. Drop by drop, it anoints the *lingam*. This water is supremely sacred. It destroys the fear of having to take birth again and again. It is the holy Ganges, which flows from Lord Shiva's locks. It is said that a drop of this water will surely fall on the palm of one with whom Shiva is pleased.

Later on, devotees came to bathe in the hot springs and then to offer fruits and flowers and do *abhishek*, the ritual bath, to Bhagawan Nityananda. On certain auspicious days — on Mondays in the month of Shravan, in the rainy season, and on Shivaratri — brahmin priests recite Vedic mantras and perform special pujas and *abhisheks*. On those occasions the entire surroundings reverberate with the divine sound of mantras.

Next to the temple are three hot springs known as *bhīmkundas*, which are considered especially sacred. During the very early hours of the morning, Shree Gurudev used to take long baths in these springs. Devotees would come secretly and watch him, and after this special darshan they would feel very happy. Gurudev attached great importance to the waters of these springs. He would often ask people who came for his darshan if they had been to the baths. To people with stomachaches and fevers, he would say, "Go and bathe in the hot springs. They contain all medicines." Through his grace, many devotees for whom he prescribed these baths were cured of diseases thought to be incurable.

At the beginning of his time in Ganeshpuri, Shree Gurudev lived in a small rest house that he built near the hot springs. His presence there was a strong support for the villagers. As people watched his work unfold and saw how remarkable it was, they told others, and so in a natural way his fame spread.

In those days there was no place for visitors to stay. Even so, people sought him out. They came from Bombay and from farther away as well. Eventually the road to Ganeshpuri was paved, and more and more people came from towns and cities to have the darshan of Bhagawan Nityananda.

Later, some devotees built a larger place for him to stay, called Kailas Nivas, and he agreed to move there from the little rest house by the hot springs. Then it was easier for visitors and for the regular devotees to come for satsang and to have his darshan.

Thanks to Gurudev's grace, today there are many facilities for visitors in Ganeshpuri. There are rest houses, several hotels, shops for food and clothing, a tailor, a laundry, and a clinic. Gurudev had a power station constructed. In time, there was a regular bus service from Thane, Vasai, and Virar. A number of townspeople have built bungalows in the area; the development is known as Nityananda Colony.

A breakfast program was established to provide food every morning to poor children from nearby villages, and later a primary school was built.

HIS APPEARANCE
AND DAILY ACTIVITIES

My Gurudev's form was supremely radiant and attractive, and if a person had his darshan even once, the impression would be deeply and unforgettably imprinted on his mind.

His skin was like a dark shining jewel filled with divine radiance. His forehead was high and arched, and his face completely captivating. Thick eyebrows curved over his large beautiful eyes. A river of love poured forth from his glance. His ears had the graceful shape of conch shells. Most of the time his attention was turned inward, as he sat peacefully with a smile on his lotus face.

Gurudev loved solitude. He was utterly content; a perfect renunciant; free from desire of any kind, free from any sense of lack. He was unique. His inner state was always blissful, and that joy played across his features. Now and then he would laugh out loud, and the sound of that laughter still rings in the ears of those lucky enough to have heard it. He was — as his name says — always joyful.

The scriptures speak of Krishna, who came to this earth with a discus, Ram with a bow, Parashurama with a battle axe, and Balaram with a plough. Shree Gurudev came with only a loincloth.

His way of life was extremely simple. He would bathe very early in the morning, before sunrise. He ate very little. His simplicity and renunciation revealed the greatness of his inner state.

Most of the time Gurudev was silent. However, if someone asked him a question, he would explain abstract philosophy in very simple words that were immediately understood. He knew several languages: Hindi, Marathi, English, Kannada, Telugu, Tamil, and Malayalam. Sometimes he recited very beautiful Sanskrit verses.

He lived beyond the *turīya* state in a supremely blissful, exalted state that is free from dreams, delusions of hope, sorrow, want, laziness, and any kind of expectation. The *Māndūkya Upanishad* describes this state as:

adrishtam avyavahāryam agrāhyam alakshanam
achintyam avyapadeshyam ekātma-pratyayāsāram
prapañchopashamam shāntam shiva advaitam chaturtham
manyante sa ātmā sa vijñeyah / [1:7]

It cannot be seen or spoken about or grasped;
it has no distinctive marks; it is unthinkable and indescribable;
it is the essence of Consciousness,
manifesting as the Self in which all phenomena subside;
tranquil, blissful, and nondual —
this is the Self, and this is what has to be realized.

HIS EFFECT ON PEOPLE

Shree Gurudev was one with God, and in his company a person could experience God directly. Anyone who had his darshan felt that he belonged to Gurudev. After that experience, it was not really possible to leave him because Gurudev existed as the inner Self in everyone. With his darshan, all the difficulties and worries of the world would disappear. A person could transcend his troubles and attain lasting happiness by coming to the sacred land of Ganeshpuri, practicing devotion to Gurudev and having faith in his greatness.

The devotees addressed him lovingly as "Baba." They loved him so much that they would stand in the darshan line for hours in the hot sun or pouring rain and never feel tired. They felt very fortunate if they could have even a glimpse of him or perhaps receive a glance from him. Whoever saw him had the feeling that Baba was his and knew all his difficulties. The inner state of such devotees was like that of the *gopīs* described in the *Shrīmad Bhāgavatam*. In the famous drama described in that scripture, even though there were many *gopīs*, each one felt that Lord Krishna was dancing just with her, that he belonged to her alone.

The devotees' love for Gurudev and their faith in him made sorrow and pain disappear. For such dear devotees, Shree Gurudev had turned Ganeshpuri into a heavenly kingdom, and he himself was the king. People spoke of him all through the village. Through his happiness, they were happy. They rejoiced in his joy and were distressed if he was ill. Shree Gurudev lived for the sake of his beloved devotees. He was moved by their love, and he cured their pain and sorrow. A devotee who offered his whole being to Gurudev would find himself totally protected by him. In his company, seekers found deep contentment and satisfaction. In his presence, knots of doubt and confusion would unravel and disappear.

In the *Mundaka Upanishad* it is said:

bhidyate hridaya-granthish chidyante sarva-samshayāh /
kshīyante chāsya karmāni tasmin drishte parāvare // [2.1:9]

The knot of ignorance in the heart is untied,
all doubts are dissolved,
and the consequences of all actions disappear
when the Lord is seen.

In Shree Gurudev's powerful presence, those who had questions would become silent. Sometimes they would receive answers to those unasked questions in mysterious ways, through a gesture or a cryptic word from him. He spoke very little, but whatever he said was infused with profound meaning. Often he communicated with his eyes. Sometimes he would ask devotees whether they had eaten or whether they had bathed in the hot springs. Just hearing these few words, they would feel delight. Occasionally, Gurudev would give sweets or fruit to someone as *prasād*, a gift that carries blessings. Whoever received *prasād* from him would consider himself the most blessed person on this earth. In the *Shrīmad Bhāgavatam*, the sage Shukadev says that to have the darshan of a great being is very rare, and that to receive *prasād* from such a being destroys all sorrow and suffering.

Devotees from the city forgot all their worldly problems when they arrived in Ganeshpuri. They came on weekends, and during those two days would soak up enough peace and contentment to last for the next five days when they returned to their everyday lives. Just as birds return to their nest at the end of the day and find peace, in the same way worldly people returned on weekends to find peace in the presence of Shree Gurudev. Some devotees settled down in his company forever.

Shree Gurudev stayed at Kailas Nivas but the entire area was permeated by his presence. He used to say, "Be calm — I am everywhere." Every devotee had his own personal experiences with Gurudev, and if all their stories were collected, it would make a very thick book. Yet Gurudev himself sat very simply on a blanket spread on a stone platform within the four walls of Kailas Nivas. From there, he cared for devotees near and far.

In Baba's kingdom the *adivasis*, the tribal people of Ganeshpuri and the surrounding villages, had no shortage of food and clothing. Gurudev was the support of their lives, and he himself would distribute the food and clothing to them. At such times the children would cry out, "Baba, Baba" in delight, and

the sound of their voices would echo through Kailas Nivas. Sometimes Gurudev would roam around with the children in a state of pure delight.

HIS LOVE
FOR CHILDREN

Shree Gurudev had great love for children. He used to say that children have very little attachment and aversion, and that they are reflections of God. For this reason he always enjoyed giving them sweets and cookies and clothes and other gifts. The children of the neighborhood usually spent their time near him, and all day long Kailas Nivas was full of the sounds of children playing. Gurudev kept many different toys for them. He also provided them with food. Every day some thousand to fifteen hundred children had their morning meal in the children's dining room. From time to time clothes were distributed as well. Even today, this work goes on: the poor children of the villages are served a meal every morning. Similarly, *sādhus*, monks, and other seekers were always treated as guests and offered food. Shree Gurudev's instruction was, "Understand that food is God."

OFFERINGS

Thousands of people came for Shree Gurudev's darshan, and the gifts they brought were an expression of their devotion and feeling toward him. According to the scriptures, there are four kinds of beings one should never approach empty-handed: gods, Gurus, kings, and children. And so people came with offerings. They brought sweets, fruits, cookies, tins of peppermint. City dwellers would bring clothing: *dhotis* and saris, caps for the children, underwear, and shirts. They brought slates and pens and books; they brought umbrellas and blankets. So plentiful were the gifts that it looked like a small market had sprung up around Gurudev. These goods were of no interest to him — he was completely content with his loincloth — but because all people were equal in his eyes and because he loved them all, he would welcome each person with love and accept his or her gift. From time to time he would have the gifts distributed among children and the poor.

BOWING TO HIM

Whoever came for Gurudev's darshan would bow to him and pay his respects in his own way, and then sit down. Some of the so-called sophisticated visitors looked down upon this practice, thus revealing that they were mean-hearted, small-minded, and ignorant. The scriptures condemn those who are unwilling to bow to their elders, to Gurus, and to images of gods and goddesses. There is nothing humiliating or demeaning in bowing down before the Guru. Even Lord Rama himself bowed down to touch the feet of sages and Masters. A noble person regards others as greater than he, and he shows his greatness by bowing to them.

To greet each other respectfully is to begin to know each other. In fact, to respect one another is to follow the dharma of the Vedas. Shree Gurudev used to say, "All is Brahman; everything is God!" When someone said to him, "O Bhagawan, O Lord, I bow to you," he retorted, "You yourself are the Lord, and all these other people are also the Lord."

When people bow to each other, God is worshiping Himself. The supreme Lord, who is Existence, Consciousness, and Bliss, dwells in every form. He is the same essence within different forms.

The yogic scriptures say that a tremendous Shakti flows through the feet of great beings and that it is transmitted through contact. The touch of this Shakti is very beneficial and brings great fortune to whoever receives it.

IN HIS ASHRAM

Shree Gurudev loved to be very sparing in his speech, and most of the time he was silent. When a person has realized the essence of the Vedas, he becomes peaceful, silent, and thought-free. After realization, this entire world appears as an illusion, and there are no activities left to undertake. Talking about the illusory world becomes a waste. For this reason Shree Gurudev observed silence for long periods. So powerful was his peacefulness and detachment that whoever sat in his company would also become silent and still.

There is an aphorism in the *Rig Veda* that says: "Only one who obeys can command." In the same way, it was only because Gurudev was established in a calm and thought-free state that he was able to give that experience to others. The state he lived in — steady and wordless — was a powerful example. Similarly, whoever spent time near Shree Gauranga Prabhu, another great being, became intoxicated with ecstasy. It is said that whoever came close to Lord Buddha would become nonviolent. In his presence the cow and tiger sat peacefully next to each other. The Puranas describe a great being named Kakabhushandi who used to repeat the name of Rama continuously. The atmosphere in his ashram became so permeated with the name of Ram that people coming for darshan would merge into the name of the Lord. Similarly, Shree Gurudev, through his detachment, was absorbed in pure Consciousness. Because of this, all kinds of people around him experienced peace and stillness.

The atmosphere around Shree Gurudev was very disciplined. He used to recommend different paths to different seekers, depending on their capacity and temperament. For himself, though, he loved silence and meditation. He would sit in his place, tranquil and silent, and all the people who sat with him were silent too.

CHAPTER THREE

Devotion and the Lord

Salutations to the Sadguru,
who is dearest among the gods.
Remover of sorrows, giver of happiness and peace,
you destroy all fears, and so grant fearlessness.
You are supremely dear to our hearts;
you kindle the highest inspiration,
and you are the focus of our loving feelings.
Sometimes you teach us righteousness;
sometimes meditation;
sometimes you teach us devotion; sometimes wisdom.
You impart the name of the Lord.
Your nature is love itself.
O Gurudev, you are the protector of our spiritual
and material life.

Each person understands another according to his capacity, his purity of heart, and his intellect. This is what Eknath Maharaj says in the *Bhavārtha Rāmāyana*. Take the case of Lord Rama.

Demons knew him as their enemy. Kings saw him as a brave emperor. Pure-hearted devotees of God felt he was God incarnate and worthy of worship. Siddhas and seers, whose minds are totally clear, perceived Lord Rama as the supreme Purusha, the Self of all. Many people saw him as the one indwelling Spirit, permeating every creature and every object.

Whatever one knows is colored by his inner state, his feeling, and is filtered through his personal history, his good and bad actions. Even so, a person can delude himself into thinking that his limited perception is the absolute Truth. In reality, it is only when the heart is purified and God reveals Himself within, that a person knows directly what is true and what is not true.

PERCEPTIONS
OF THE DEVOTEES

A person's feelings are influenced by those around him. Then these feelings create thoughts, and the thoughts produce a state of mind, and the state of mind gives rise to questions. So a person asks questions according to his feelings.

Those who follow the path of devotion, *bhaktas*, would come to Bhagawan Nityananda and ask, "O Sir, are you a *bhakta*?"

"Yes," he would say.

Followers of *ashtānga yoga* would ask him, "Babaji, are you a yogi?"

"Yes," he would answer.

Vedantins, those who pursue the path of knowledge, would ask, "Swamiji, are you a *jñāni*, a knower of the Truth?"

"Yes," Gurudev would reply.

And with that, they would argue with each other. The first said, "I asked him and he said he was a *bhakta*." The second, "I asked him too, and he's a great yogi." And the third, "No, he's a knower of the Truth; he's a *jñāni*." In this way, they would debate and each would argue his own point of view.

The fact is that Bhagawan Nityananda was all of these — he was a *bhakta*, a yogi, and a *jñāni*. He contained everything. But who can really understand this? How could there be yoga, union with the Divine, without devotion? How could there be pure knowledge without yoga? How could one realize the divine essence without having attained pure knowledge? How could one attain pure knowledge and lasting bliss without God-realization? Are supreme bliss and Nityananda different? In reality, it is impossible to separate devotion, union with God, and knowledge.

Bhakti means love, and love is only another name for joy. Joy arises when the restlessness of the mind is stilled. Creating a still mind is called yoga. Through yoga, knowledge arises.

The idea of yoga makes many people uneasy. They think yoga means turning your back on the world, living in a mountain cave, and eating wild roots and berries. But this is not so.

Every soul in this world practices yoga to some extent. A person follows certain rules of conduct (*yama-niyama*): regularity in getting up, eating, getting to work, and going to bed. Whatever kind of work one does requires concentration (*dhyāna*). A painting, for instance, becomes beautiful through the artist's concentration. In the same way, everyone has some experience of love (*prema*), devotion (*bhakti*), and knowledge (*jñāna*) — everyone feels devoted to someone or other. Through discrimination (*viveka*), one distinguishes between good and bad. So devotion, yoga, and knowledge are all essential and interwoven parts of life. That is why Shree Gurudev would answer "yes" to all those questions.

HIS EQUANIMITY

*B*hagawan Nityananda had equal vision. He treated all people alike, regardless of their color, their importance in the world, their education. Rich and poor, educated and illiterate — all of them were the same in Gurudev's eyes. For him, this entire universe was a reflection of the same divine Self. He used to say that the world is a play of Consciousness. Just as many kinds of ornaments, bracelets, rings, and earrings are made from the same gold; just as many different sizes and shapes of pots are made from the same clay; and just as various kinds of cloth are made from the same thread; in the same way, this entire universe of myriad forms is made of the same divine Consciousness. Therefore, Shree Gurudev said, "Have the same feeling of love for everyone as you have for your own Self."

Many kinds of people used to come to Bhagawan Nityananda. Every day there was a new group of pilgrims. Whether they were ascetics or mendicants, monks or heads of ashrams; whether they were Christian priests or followers of Madhavacharya or yogis from Himalayan caves, Gurudev saw all of them in the same way. For him, all religions were equal. He saw all sects, all ideologies, and all philosophies as equal. He used to say that each sect or doctrine or creed is a different path leading to the same goal. Many paths lead to the same destination. You can reach Bombay via Poona or Nasik, or by sea or air. Similarly, through all these different philosophies one can attain the same divine state.

The world is made by God, but religions and sects and doctrines are made by man. Gurudev used to say that for everything, whether animate or inanimate, there is the same earth and air and water, the same sun and moon and sky, the same heaven and hell, the same God and Guru. The same earth supports every creature. The same air flows through the *prāna* of all beings. The same water gives life to people and plants. Man existed before any religion or ideology, and it was man who established the different doctrines and beliefs and scriptures. But for all people, regardless of what they call Him, God is one.

In the court of Shree Gurudev, people of different religions — Hindus, Muslims, Sikhs, Parsis, Christians, Jews, and Jains — would throng around him. He was adored by those who believed in God and by those who did not. He was dearly loved by all.

For Gurudev, all forms of worship were equivalent. He had the same respect for all of them. He saw no difference between God manifested in form and God in the abstract. He used to say that the same God dwells in different forms, just as the same material is used in different buildings — in the Shiva temples of the Shaivites, the Vishnu temples of the Vaishnavas, the Jain temples, the Christian churches, and the Muslim mosques. In all these places, people perform worship through various rituals or hymns or chants or prayers, and they all receive satisfaction. The satisfaction, the joy, the ecstasy, the state of liberation they experience is the same. The attainment is the same. There are differences in the forms of worship and in the individual, but not in their attainment and not in God.

Where does the difference lie — in man or in God? God is the same; it is only people in their ignorance who see differences. In God there are no differences; there is no hatred, no jealousy, no distinction between big and small, high and low, no pride in belief or religion.

In the *Bhagavad Gītā*, Lord Krishna says:

samo'ham sarvabhūteshu na me dveshyo'sti na priyah / [9:29]

I am equally present in all beings;
none are disliked by Me or dear to Me.

It is He whose spirit manifests in all living beings, and in His eyes:

mayā tatam idam sarvam jagad avyaktamūrtinā / [9:4]

This whole universe is permeated by Me
in my unmanifest aspect.

Similarly, Bhagawan Nityanandaji, in a state of ecstatic joy, would sometimes say, "I am in everything; everything is in me."

THE COURT
OF THE GURU

All kinds of people used to come to Shree Gurudev — prominent leaders and government officials, engineers, doctors and lawyers, pundits and scholars, yogis, *mahātmas*, seekers, *jñānis*, poets and musicians, researchers, rich men and beggars, the unhappy, the sick, landowners and laborers, actors and actresses, monks and nuns, the well-behaved, the intelligent and the stupid, also wicked people, thieves, and hunters — in short, every type of person who lives in this world came to Bhagawan Nityananda. Since every kind of person under the sun was there, it seemed to be the Lord's own congregation.

I once met a learned pundit who said to me, "Swami, your

Gurudev's court must be the court of God Himself because so many different kinds of people could live together only where the Lord dwells."

Even so, various arguments and conflicts took place. This is nothing to be surprised at — there should be room for everything in the court of God. If something were missing, it would reflect on God's fullness and completeness. Many devotees used to criticize these happenings and the people involved in them. They would ask why such people — foolish, sinful, dirty, bad-mannered, and wicked — came to Gurudev. Even today, the same kind of question is raised over and over again.

The answer to the question is found in the example of the river Ganges. The Ganges purifies everyone, from the virtuous to the evil. She has only one quality, and it is divine. Anyone — a *sādhu* or a sinner — can bathe in her holy waters and be purified. A sacred cow comes and drinks the cool water and becomes still. A tiger comes, slakes his thirst, and also becomes calm. Both the tiger and the cow enjoy the same refreshing coolness. In the Ganges there is equanimity and love; she treats everyone alike. She takes no notice of the good or bad qualities of those who come to her. She seems to say, "Come. Be purified. Become still, and then go."

But people like to make judgments, to speak of good and bad, merit and demerit, success and failure. In an engineering college, only engineering students are admitted; in a medical school, only medical students. But everyone is welcome in God's court, in the Guru's court, because it is a community where everyone can learn. This is how it was in the court of Shree Nityanandaji.

This reminds me of a story about King Akbar. One day the king asked Birbal, his prime minister, "O minister, tell me who is greater — God or me?"

Now, Birbal was a very intelligent man and he knew just how to handle delicate situations.

"O king, you are greater!" replied the prime minister.

The king was pleased. "Now, tell me, how am I greater than God?"

Birbal was ready with the answer. "O king, if anyone commits a crime in your kingdom or goes against your wishes, you can easily have him removed from your kingdom. But if someone commits a crime or goes against the will of God, He is powerless to have him removed from His kingdom — which is the universe."

"Very good," said the king. "That's exactly right."

The point is that foolish people make judgments and argue. They say, "You are good; come here" or "You are bad; go away." If a person's understanding is imperfect, his behavior will be too. But one who is above good and bad, one who dwells in a state of purity is like God Himself. He loves everyone. Everyone belongs to him, and he belongs to everyone. Gurudev was a *mahātma*, a great being, who lived in this pure state. That is why all kinds of people were drawn to him.

Everyone needs the water of the Ganges: deities, monks, saints and devotees, benefactors, kings and beggars, sinners, thieves, animals, birds, and wild creatures. Water is life. In the same way, everyone needs great beings. They dwell in this world for the good of all. In their presence, a scholar and a fool both become peaceful. That is why in Bhagawan Nityananda's court there were people of every kind. He existed for everyone and everyone was his.

In arithmetic, it is the numbers that create value. If you write a zero after the number one, you have ten. If you write two zeroes, you have a hundred; three zeroes and you have a thousand. The only thing that gives value to the zeroes is the one. If you remove all the zeroes, the one is still there. In the same way, it is because of God that everything else exists and has value.

An artist uses color to paint different forms on canvas: cows and tigers, rivers and mountains, houses and trees. Similarly, God has created this infinitely varied universe with His sublime skill. He exists as the Consciousness that pervades everything, that invents infinite colors and generates marvelous forms — all for the sake of love and beauty and joy. Everything that exists is for giving satisfaction to the inner Self. It is not for enmity or hatred, not for proving blame in innocence or innocence in blame.

Bhagawan Nityananda used to say, "This universe is infinite and it is your own Self. See the world as a form of the inner Self. The world is not separate from you and you are not separate from the world. This is Vedanta, this is devotion, and this is worship. Dwelling right within you is your own Lord."

THE CRY
OF THE DEVOTEE

*A*lways, Bhagawan Nityananda was tranquil and ecstatic, absorbed in pure knowledge and divine love. Whoever came to him saw in him a reflection of his own feelings. Because of this, a strong awareness would arise in everyone's heart: "My inner Self is the same as Shree Nityananda."

Gurudev was utterly free of desire and that attracted people irresistibly. People came to him seeking fulfillment of all kinds of desires — even though he was free of desires himself.

A seeker full of devotion would come and say, "Maharaj, you are one with God. Give me liberation!"

A well-educated person would approach and say, "Swamiji, you are one with God. Give me that pure knowledge!"

Yet another would say, "Babaji, I don't want anything — just give me a little love!" Although such a seeker said he didn't want anything, in fact he had an underlying desire for that supreme blissful love, which is the foundation of the Truth.

Seeing these dramas go on, Gurudev would smile and say yes to all the requests.

Years ago I used to visit Pandharpur. There was a Siddha there called Narasimha Swami. We had a very loving relationship, and I would visit there several times a year. I love Pandharpur very much. Every day huge crowds of people went to the Pandharinath Temple. All kinds of people came for the darshan of Pandharinath Vithobaji: devotees, Siddhas, the learned, the literate and illiterate, those who loved the world and those who had renounced it, the sick, the sinful and the virtuous, maharajas and ordinary people. They came to pray to that ancient and powerful image of the Lord who has been worshiped in Pandharpur for so long.

At Pandharpur I witnessed on a smaller scale the same kind of scene that I would see in Ganeshpuri. In Bhagawan Nityananda's court there were crowds every day. Some people would ask for knowledge. Others asked for wealth, a house, a job. Many women would come to Gurudev. One might say, "Bhagawan, I have no children. Please grant me a child." Another would say, "Bhagawan, I have six daughters! Now grant me a son." Gurudev would respond, "Yes, have faith. You will have everything." This was the daily drama that was enacted around him.

A devotee might tell him, "Babaji, every day I offer worship to Shree Datta. Yesterday when I was doing *āratī* to his statue, I saw you! So today I came running here!"

Another would say, "Bhagawan, a week ago you came to me in a vision and said, 'Bring fifty pounds of ladus and feed the children. Then all your worries will leave you.' So here are the ladus that I have brought!"

A third person would tell him, "Yesterday you appeared in my dream and said, 'You will get a job — go.' So should I go?" Babaji would answer, "Yes." Then that man would leave and find a job.

There were endless incidents like these. Seeing them happen and hearing about them, seekers found their devotion and faith refreshed and strengthened. Their hearts wanted to reach out and hug Gurudev tightly. Their feeling of devotion made them want to bow to him again and again.

HIS OMNISCIENCE

The pure sages who know Vedanta have said that the source of this world is Brahman. Everything was created out of Brahman, and that one supreme Consciousness became everything — good people and bad, kings and their subjects, gods and sages, and all the myriad thousands of life forms. The universe is Brahman: its Creator is Brahman and what He created is also Brahman. In the *Bhagavad Gītā*, Lord Krishna says:

mattah parataram nānyat kinchid asti dhananjaya / [7:7]

There is nothing other than Me, O Arjuna.

The one who gives is Brahman and the one who takes is also Brahman; the one who is eating is Brahman and the one who is preparing food is Brahman; the one asking for alms and the one giving in charity are Brahman. The one who is writing this and the one who is reading this are Brahman. Brahman permeates everything.

In spite of this, people experience many different feelings — happiness, frustration, and so on. Because of their temperaments, they like certain things, even though they may not be at all beneficial. Similarly, because of their inclinations and tastes, they dislike other things which may be valuable. Everyone in the world has his own particular preferences. Only a very rare person knows the Truth in its real form.

People would ask Bhagawan Nityananda for various things, depending on their inclinations. If someone asked for the blessing of a child, someone else with other interests might laugh and make fun of him, saying, "Did you know that he asked Bhagawan for a child?" But Shree Gurudev was the Self of all. He knew everyone's mind, and therefore he never made fun of anyone but gave to each person what he wanted.

When someone came to him asking to be cured of a disease, Gurudev would never tell him to seek spiritual attainment instead. If someone lacking understanding criticized such a person, Gurudev would not say anything but remain silent.

Imagine that a man is making a long journey by car. The car breaks down and he discovers that he needs a steel part to repair it. He asks where the nearest garage is so he can get the steel part. A bystander says, "Why are you buying steel? There's a jewelry store right over there and they have gold and silver. You should buy gold instead!" Then the driver gets angry and says, "What are you talking about? I'm just trying to get my car fixed!"

Shree Gurudev would give the person what he asked for. In his eyes, the same pure Self existed in everyone and there was no such notion as high and low. For him, everything contained the Self.

CHAPTER FOUR

ℋ Supreme Avadhūt

ℋe bears no malice toward the world;
he has no desire, not even for Self-realization.
The world does not exist for him;
the Self is what is real to him,
and he dwells in that Self.
He sees the Self pervading everywhere.
With no awareness of his physical body,
completely fulfilled within his own Self,
such a being is an avadhūt.

Gurudev Shree Nityanandaji was a realized being; he was one with Brahman. Deeply rooted and absorbed in God, he nevertheless worked actively for the benefit of his devotees. His senses were naturally turned within. His eyes were half open but his vision was not attracted to outer forms or qualities. With his attention focused inward, he would rest in the light of the inner Self. This is how the *Hatha Yoga Pradīpīka* describes it:

antar-laksyo bahir-dristir-nimesonmesa-varjita / [4:36]

This describes the *shāmbhavī mudrā* as "Attention turned inward, gaze outward, without any blinking of the eyes." Gurudev was often in this state.

A great saint, Tukaram Maharaj, says:

visaya to tyancha jhala narayana /

His one and only passion was the Lord.

Shree Gurudev was constantly engrossed in the inner Self. His vision was turned inward. His hearing was merged with the great mantra, the *mahāmantra*, that underlies all sounds. His *prāna* was one with the inner aroma, and his sense of taste with the supreme nectar, the *mahārasa*, which is the source of all the sweetness in this world. In such a state, how could the senses possibly be drawn away from the ocean of inner bliss?

The Upanishads say:

raso vai sah

That indeed is pure ambrosia.

That state of Self-absorption is delicious like nectar, and full of love, full of bliss, full of happiness, full of peace. All the saints have described this inner state.

If someone who was suffering came to Bhagawan Nityananda and talked about all the things he lacked, Gurudev would say to him, "Everything is contained in your inner Self; everything is inside you. Why are you crying? Search inside; you will find everything within."

When Gurudev was deeply absorbed in the Self, it didn't matter who had come for his darshan — even some very important person — it would take him a long time to open his eyes and turn his attention outward. This was because he had gone so deep within. Yet at other times he might respond immediately to someone and say, "Everything is inside you."

Not only did he tell seekers that everything was within, Gurudev was himself a living example of this truth. He had indeed attained everything within.

Tukaram Maharaj says:

bole taisa chale tyachi vandavi paule /

Bow to one who does himself what he instructs others to do. Such a one is divine; he is God Himself.

Shree Nityanandaji was a living illustration of the truth of that teaching.

THE INNER REALM

*T*he human spirit loves certain sights, tastes, sounds, fragrances, and touches. But the happiness of the inner sensations is so much greater than the happiness of outer sensations. Everything on the outside is fully present in subtle form within. "Search inside yourself," Gurudev used to say, urging devotees to explore their own inner realms. And he himself was always absorbed within.

Inside, there is a divine light. Gazing at this lovely light, yogis forget themselves. No language, no words can really describe this exquisite light.

From one point of view, this body is a bundle of meat, full of decaying matter, ugly and impure. When a person dies and divine Consciousness leaves the body as a tiny flame, the corpse is a frightening sight to many people. Even if that body was much loved, you hate to see it after the light of Consciousness has left it. Your eyes turn away from the corpse. How beautiful that divine Consciousness must be, which made the body appear glowing and lovable, beautiful and full of goodness. How radiant that light must be, how powerful. How much sweetness it must have. All this is known by the one who has lost himself in the inner Self.

Bhagawan Nityananda used to say, "O soul, you should see the inner beauty. It is so sweet, so fascinating, so joyous. Not even a drop of that inner ocean can be found on the outside. Therefore, turn within. Meditate, meditate, meditate!" This was his message.

Another attraction of the inner world is sound. Sweet words are very dear to everyone. Birds in the forest tell their stories with their own sweet sounds. Within us is a divine sound known as *nāda*. This inner music is irresistible, it is lovable. It echoes in the inner space. Yogis take the help of this inner music to make themselves one with the Self. *Nāda* brings divine bliss. It is a potent way of focusing on the supreme Lord. There are different kinds of *nāda*, and the scriptures say if you listen to it properly, your pain and suffering will burn away and you will be free of any darkness. Through this inner music, you can attain the transcendent state. A seeker who loses himself in it merges with God. Bhagawan Nityananda used to say, "What is outer music? Listen to the inner music. It contains supreme contentment; it is the music of the Self. Turn your mind within and listen!"

The third subtle sense that appeals from the inside is *rasa*, or taste. It offers sensations of exquisite flavor. While listening to *nāda*, the mind is concentrated at the root of the inner ear, and the tongue is drawn upward and clings to the palate. Then, because of the inner joy, a spring of *amrit*, nectar, flows from the *sahasrāra*, the thousand-petaled lotus at the crown of the head. Even a tiny drop of this nectar has such extraordinary sweetness that it surpasses all the sweets in the outer world. Bhagawan Nityananda used to say, "Drink this nectar; it is the flavor of the inner Self."

Then there is the inner aroma. When the mind and *prāna* of yogis become focused on the *ājñā chakra*, between the eyebrows, they can experience the divine fragrance. Even other people who are nearby can sometimes smell the sublime fragrance emanating from such yogis.

The fifth treasure within us is the sense of touch. When the heart *chakra* is opened, the *prāna* spreads bliss through every pore of the body. Then one experiences the joy of this divine touch. It makes a yogi wild with delight; he dances and leaps with joy. Brimming over with intense love and with all his desires completely fulfilled, he marvels at his good fortune.

Always, Bhagawan Nityananda would say to his devotees, "All your joys are inside you in their fullness."

THE SUBLIME STATE

*T*here is no end to Shree Gurudev's greatness and inner wealth. One can think of him as a simple being like us, but in his pure state he was merged with God and had manifested in a human body. With this understanding it becomes clear that Gurudev is beyond description. But since the mind needs the satisfaction of defining him in some way, it can be said that Gurudev was a supreme *avadhūt*.

Shree Gurudev was always awake. No one ever saw him sleep. Sometimes I stayed at his Vaikuntha Ashram for many days, but I never saw him sleep. I have heard various saints say that great beings do not sleep, that Siddhas have gone beyond the state of sleep. The Vedas describe the four states that every human being has, and they can be experienced directly: the waking state, dream state, deep-sleep state, and transcendent state, *turīya*.

The waking state consists of all the activities that take place in and through the physical body. These activities arise from the five elements, the five senses of perception, the five organs of action, and the four aspects of the mind. The dream state occurs in the subtle body. The deep-sleep state takes place in the causal body.

Everyone has experienced these three states. But beyond these is a fourth state, called *turīya* or the transcendent state. Yogis learn to go past the causal body and live in the supracausal body of this *turīya* state. And even beyond this is the *turīyātita* state, which is the state of the Siddhas. It is beyond description. It is said in the *Brihajjabal Upanishad*:

> *yatra na suryas-tapati yatra na vayur-vati yatra*
> *na chandrama bhati yatra na naksatrani bhanti yatra*
> *nagnir-dahati yatra na mrityuh pravisati yatra na duhkhani*
> *pravisanti sad-anandam paramanandam satyam sasvatam*
> *sadasivam brahmadi-vanditam yogi-dhyeyam param padam*
> *yatra gatva na nivartante yoginah* [8:6]

> It is beyond the heat of the sun, the blowing of the wind,
> and the coolness of the moon;
> beyond starlight and the blaze of fire;
> beyond pain and death.
> It is supremely blissful, eternal, and peaceful.

This supremely beneficial state contains total freedom, complete liberation. It is the state of Shiva, of the Lord, and it is attainable through the practice of Maha Yoga, the great yoga. The seeker, utterly transformed, has a constant experience of God. This is the final attainment of the great sages, obtained through austerities. Once this goal is attained, it is never lost. Shree Nityanandaji lived in this sublime state. One who dwells here is called an *avadhūt*.

Shree Gurudev lived in Ganeshpuri where the three seasons are extreme: the summer is very hot, the monsoon has very heavy rains, and the winter is very cold. Even so, Gurudev lived the same way throughout the year. The weather never bothered him. Neither heat nor cold had any effect on him. He had infinite self-control. He used to say it is the mind that experiences happiness and sorrow, and that all seasons are alike for one who has transcended body-consciousness.

His All-Pervasiveness

Shree Gurudev pervaded everyone in equal measure. This entire world consists of different forms of God. Yogis who have attained complete knowledge say this world is a play of God, and He can be seen in every part of it. The world is not a solid substance, not the final reality; it is a form of the Self, a play of divine Consciousness, a symbol of joy. Marveling at this cosmic drama, some have called the Lord a master of disguise, a supreme actor who can play any role, because even though He is one and indivisible, He reveals Himself in millions of forms, and through maya He takes part in every play. Though inactive, He appears to be active. The delusions of maya, and maya herself, are also forms of the Lord. All this is His amazing composition, His mysterious creation. Even though He is free, He assumes a body. Though He is the giver of all, He takes on the form of a beggar and eats whatever is given in charity. The only One dwelling in this entire world is God. In Him lies the ever-changing drama of this astounding world. Just as from gold many different ornaments are created, just as from clay many different pots and vessels are shaped, and just as from a drop of semen comes a human body with many different organs, similarly, the whole world is a form of God. And Shree Gurudev pervades all of it.

"I am in everything," he used to say to people coming for darshan. Once a photographer asked permission to take his picture.

"Take a picture of the world," replied Gurudev. "I am the world. Is there any place where I don't exist? In everything, there is a glimpse of me." The world is one with Nityananda, and Nityananda pervades the entire world.

Bhagawan Nityananda was a perfect Master of yoga. Always he reveled in his own joy, knowing that in the whole world there was nothing different from him. Whatever the time or circumstances, he could be seen in the same ecstatic state, the inner awareness that "This whole world is my play." Such was the pulsating, scintillating experience in which he lived.

Since he saw neither faults nor virtues, he saw nothing to reject and nothing to accept. So amazing was Shree Gurudev's detachment that even though he saw, he appeared not to see; even though he heard, he appeared not to hear; and even though he spoke, it seemed that he didn't speak. His mind was free of qualities and attributes. This is why he was neither a doer nor an enjoyer, neither a receiver nor a giver, neither happy nor unhappy, neither with desire nor without it, neither a king nor a beggar, neither awake nor asleep, neither omniscient nor limited in knowledge — he was beyond all dualities, established in the state of supreme freedom. He was a Siddha. His nature was pure Consciousness, illumined by the light of the Self.

CHAPTER FIVE

The Work of the Siddha Guru

Drunk with ignorance,
you have forgotten your true Self.
Completely immersed in worldly pleasures,
you are trapped in the cycle of birth and death.
Hail to the one who gives the vision of the Self,
which is beyond this ignorance.
Hail to that Shree Gurudev, destroyer of all sins,
who delivers us from the world.

The lives of saints are rich and inscrutable. Their mystery cannot be unraveled by mere words. Siddhas live in unpredictable ways. Their behavior seems mysterious and puzzling, but everything they do is for the upliftment of humanity. They exist in this difficult world to bring happiness and fulfillment to mankind.

Tukaram Maharaj, a great saint, said:

panyamadhye masa jhopa gheto kaisa /
jarve tyachya vamsa tevaha kale //

To understand how a fish sleeps in water, you have to become a fish. Similarly, to understand saints and great beings, you have to experience their inner state.

Without such personal experience, trying to explain or judge great beings is foolish and childish. It shows neither intelligence nor understanding. If someone who had never been to India were sitting in England, how could he hope to describe the Taj Mahal?

DARSHAN
WITH GURUDEV

Some people used to ask why Shree Gurudev did not come out from his four walls and engage in social work with people who were confused and suffering. This question came from ignorance, which is why the work of great beings is often misunderstood.

The sun does not leave its place, yet it illumines the world. The moon does not leave its place and go from house to house, yet it showers the nectar of coolness. The sacred Ganges stays in its own place and offers refreshing water for travelers. To recognize the benefit of these holy waters, deep faith is required. In the same way, to understand the work of Siddhas, deep feeling must arise in a devotee's heart, and for this, a spiritual eye is necessary.

It is said:

na kasthe vidyate devo na pasane na kardame /
bhavesu vartate devas-tasmad-bhavam na samtyajet //

The deity worshiped through the image does not reside in the wood or stone or clay of which the image is made, but in the feeling of the worshiper. For this reason the feeling of devotion must never be given up.

The impact on the outer world of Shree Gurudev's uplifting work was secret and subtle. In contrast, the effect on people's minds was obvious — thousands came away from him saying that their minds had become still and peaceful after having his darshan. Listening to thousands of lectures and studying thousands of books cannot bring happiness, but a single gracious glance from

Bhagawan Nityananda brought happiness to many people. Whoever he might be — someone important in the eyes of the world or someone unknown — a person would come away from Gurudev's darshan with the happy feeling that whatever was lost had been found. He would feel contentment and peace of a kind never found in his everyday life in the world. After having darshan, a seeker felt that all his hopes and aspirations would be fulfilled if he sought refuge at the feet of Bhagawan Nityananda. Nourished and strengthened by him, seekers regarded him as their very life.

Shree Gurudev was a spiritual resting place. In his presence, agitation gave way to peace. The mind became utterly still; no ripple of distress remained. He was like a lake of cool, clear water, refreshing the tired traveler. The cool purity of clear water is bound to calm a disturbed mind, since purity creates purity.

As soon as the bright light of the rising sun appears, birds wake up and sing, and owls turn blind and go to sleep. Sages and priests say their prayers, and thieves run away. Wax melts and clay hardens. None of these are the deliberate work of the sun, even though they happen when the sun rises. Shree Gurudev's divine state was like this. Just as only nectar flows from the moon, in the same way only bliss flows in the company of great saints who have become one with supreme bliss.

Shree Gurudev was apparently no different from the rest of humanity made of flesh and blood, but visitors would be strongly attracted by his calm and radiant face. There was no visible give and take between Gurudev and the faithful devotees who yearned for his darshan. And yet it was through darshan that contentment came. Shree Gurudev was complete bliss: he was the eternal bliss of the Upanishads, the blissful Lord of the devotees, the yogis' bliss of meditation, the philosophers' bliss of Self-realization, and the bliss of supreme Consciousness described in the Vedas.

Standing in front of Gurudev, a visitor — whether a devotee or not — would ask himself, Why am I feeling this joy? Is the source of it hidden inside me? Puzzling and pondering, he would turn within and discover that the source of that joy was indeed the Consciousness dwelling right within him. This same Consciousness permeates the world we see. Realizing this, one could understand Gurudev's feeling that the whole world was his home.

It may seem that there are different kinds of saints, but in reality their work is the same. Usually Shree Gurudev was silent. He did not preach or lecture, but the brief messages and instructions he gave in person and in dreams were full of power.

A Bridge Across the Suffering World

Our life in this world is influenced by the consequences of actions performed in many previous lifetimes. Every soul experiences the fruits of his karma. This is why many people suffer from poverty, sorrow, disease, and ignorance. This is also why others are gifted with education, wealth, perseverance, intellect, celibacy, generosity, willpower, and dedication to God. So many different kinds of people continue to take birth in this world, and the circumstances of their lives vary greatly. Equality of outer circumstances does not exist in this difficult world, and it never will.

In reality, if a person has no knowledge of the Self, even wealth and health will not satisfy him. The most powerful king is overruled by nature. He is enslaved by material forces and defeated eventually by time.

Everyone in this world has a tale of woe. Everyone is troubled by suffering, whether it is self-inflicted or comes from outside. For this reason a person searches for happiness day and night. So absorbing is this search that he forgets his true Self. As his search for happiness takes him through endless troubles, he sighs and weeps. Yielding often to temptations and then repenting, burning with desires, harassed by suffering, a human being has a difficult life. In spite of all this, he does not give up his useless way of life. Nor does he look for some way to transform it. Nor does he seek a mantra from a liberated being who has transcended all this. How strange! This is true ignorance.

Day after day the sun rises in the east and sets in the west, then travels to the east again. With one complete cycle, a day is gone. Seven days make a week and four weeks a month. In twelve months, a year is gone. In this way, a person's life is spent, and then it disappears. Along with his birth, a person brings his death into the world with him. Like a round-trip ticket, death comes with birth. A human being is born in this diverse world, experiences happiness and unhappiness, and then, weeping, returns the same way he came, with his desires unfulfilled.

Who knows how much time is left? O dear one, why are you not more conscious? Just as you are moving now irrevocably toward death, many other souls have traveled that same road. Although you have seen others die unsatisfied, there is no transformation in your own life. Even though you are being swept away by the river of illusion, you regard yourself as quite clever. You offer help to others, and yet you yourself are utterly helpless! Could anything be more astonishing than this? O dear soul, are you awake or asleep?

Only when a person truly awakens does he realize his foolishness. Shree Gurudev, who was the embodiment of compassion, encouraged souls who were suffering to turn within.

Every soul in this world is a part of the supreme Soul, and is always seeking reunion with that blissful Lord. All the knowledge in this world, all the arts and sciences, should be understood as paths to joy. Every person values happiness and joy; they are as dear as life. For the sake of joy, the wind blows; for the sake of joy, fire blazes; for the sake of joy, cool water flows and the sun rises with a million rays of light. For the sake of joy, a person does all kinds of things, not knowing that happiness lies within.

He is like the musk deer, which carries the precious fragrance in its own navel, but out of ignorance keeps searching and searching on the outside. The breeze carries the fragrance of the musk toward the mountains, and the deer runs eagerly in that direction. It runs and runs, and in the end it dies. Then the people who live in the mountains cut open the deer and remove the musk. It is the same story with a human being. In spite of everything he does, a person does not see lasting happiness. But if, by good fortune, he meets a saint, a great being, then he can become completely happy.

The scriptures describe the world as full of desires which are never fulfilled. Seeking to satisfy these desires, people marry, have children, get an education, plant a garden, and so on. But where is the fulfillment? The sages say that all these things are —

in themselves — without *rasa*, without savor, without ultimate satisfaction.

In the *Bhagavad Gītā* there are two verses in which Lord Krishna says:

duhkhālayam ashashvatam [8:15]
anityam asukham lokam [9:33]

These verses mean that this world is a transient place of suffering, where any happiness is a brief interlude.

The world is perishable and keeps on changing every moment. When the Lord hears the cries of unfulfilled souls, He has compassion and manifests in the form of great beings to give the experience of happiness to devotees. The *Shrīmad Bhāgavatam* says that after many births, when the good karma of a soul bears fruit, then a Siddha appears and skillfully reveals dharma to him.

The goal of the embodied soul is to become free of all suffering and to attain eternal bliss. According to the Vedas, the root of suffering is ignorance, lack of knowledge of the Self. People suffer because they do not know their own divine Self. All the scriptures agree on this.

The scriptures of Vedanta, which have been taught by the sages since ancient times, say that if a person were to examine his condition and delve into himself, he would soon realize that inside him is an absolute happiness, independent of anything. It is called *ātmasukha*, the happiness of the Self. This happiness is eternal. All the delights of the world are contained here. This is the fourth state, beyond the physical, subtle, and causal levels, which everyone experiences. This is the *turīya* state, which is not known to everyone. It is in this state that lasting joy is attained. There is no greater happiness. The scriptures have various names for this state: Heaven, Paradise, Vaikuntha, Kailas, and so on.

A person is born to attain this state, to experience this joy. The purpose of human birth is fulfilled here. This place, this happiness, this stage of consciousness is asleep inside a person. It is awakened through the blessings of the Guru. To acquaint us with this blissful state, God appears in the form of a great being, a Siddha.

In the *Shiva Sūtras*, the Lord says:

gururupāyah / [2:6]

The Guru is the means.

In a commentary on this verse called the *Vimarshini* it is said:

gurur-va parameshvari anugrahika shaktih

The Guru is the grace-bestowing power of the Lord.

A perfect Master, a Siddha Guru is one who has the power to transform an ordinary soul, a *jīva*, into the universal Soul, Shiva; to change a human being, a *nara*, into Narayana, the Supreme Being. Bhagawan Nityananda was such a Siddha Guru.

He was a master of yoga. He was complete. He had the power to grant his devotees' wishes. But transcending this was the rare divine power by which he would awaken the Shakti, the inner energy, of whoever remembered him with faith and complete love. Gurudev would transmit into such a seeker his own sublime state. Tukaram Maharaj says:

apanasarikhe kariti tatkala / nahi kalavela tayalagi //

The Sadguru instantly transforms his disciple into one like him. It does not take a long time to achieve that.

It is very rare for a disciple to come across such a Guru. His work is like alchemy. He is like the philosopher's stone, transmuting iron into gold, or like a sandalwood tree, making the other trees around it cool and fragrant. Such a being transmits his Shakti into the disciple, making him like his own Self. Shree Gurudev Nityananda was such a being.

Time after time, in many different forms, saints come to uplift this world. Even after meeting such extraordinary beings, some poor souls remain trapped in attachments and do not attain anything spiritually. What bad fortune they have!

Every person on this earth feels that peace, joy, enthusiasm, and inner growth are very dear to him. Every soul keeps hoping for a divine life. No one wants to become small, incomplete, or ugly. No one wishes for ignorance, stupidity, or poverty — because a human being is no different from God; he is part of Consciousness. But as a person moves through this world, he gradually forgets his own greatness. He forgets more and more. Then he needs a true path, he needs a Guru, to help him know the greatness of the Self. Without the Guru, it is very difficult to discover that inner state. Shree Gurudev was able to give seekers a life that was divine.

All over the world, one sees that actors imitate other actors, and scholars imitate other scholars. Doctors and lawyers, artisans and artists all learn from their mentors and become like them. A rich man gives away his riches or a learned man his knowledge, making someone else rich or learned. By living with a devotee of the Lord, many people have become devotees. In the company of a yogi, many have learned yoga. So to become enlightened by being with Shree Gurudev is no great wonder.

THE POWER
OF SHAKTIPAT

*D*ifferent countries have their own particular areas of expertise, fields of knowledge in which they excel. The specialty of India lies in spirituality, through which one can attain the bliss of the Self, which is immensely valuable and dear to every soul. Without the joy of the Self, there is no lasting inner peace. Until one has experienced this peace, the purpose of life remains unfulfilled. To reach the bliss of the Self, one must have an extremely capable Guru. Only after receiving the grace of such a Guru is perfection possible.

Another name for the Guru's grace is Shaktipat. Only Siddha Gurus can give Shaktipat. They have an extraordinary capability that enables a seeker to experience his or her life as divine.

It is absolutely true that unless Shaktipat is received from a thoroughly proficient Guru, a person will not be completely satisfied. He will also lack intimate knowledge of the all-pervasiveness, purity, and unity of the Supreme Reality. Shaktipat is a wonderful and mysterious spiritual process in which the Guru showers the energy of his own soul on the disciple. In the scriptures, the grace of the Self is called Shaktipat. Without the grace of the Siddhas, Shaktipat cannot take place.

Shaktipat is a vast science. It is described in minute detail in the *shivāgama* and *shaivatantra*. Books in Hindi include

Mahāyoga Vijñāna by Yogananda Brahmachari and *Yogavani* by Shree Shankar Purushottam Tirth. Books in English are *The Serpent Power* by Sir John Woodroffe and *Devatma Shakti* by Swami Vishnutirth. All these books are of help to a seeker in his sadhana, his spiritual practice. But as long as a seeker, an aspirant, has not received Shaktipat from a Guru, his spiritual journey is very difficult. Through the grace of a Siddha, however, the Self is experienced with great ease. The *Yogashikhā Upanishad* says:

nānāmārgaistu dushprāpyam kaivalyam paramam padam /
siddhimārgena labhate nānyathā padmasambhava // [1:3]

The supreme state of being established in one's own real nature, which is so difficult to attain through other means, is easily attained by the grace of a Siddha.

Shree Gurudev awakened the Kundalini Shakti in the disciple through Shaktipat. This Kundalini Shakti is the same as universal Consciousness. It is another name for the divine Consciousness that appears as the universe. This Consciousness is an independent power that makes the world appear full of differences. According to the *Pratyabhijñāhridayam*:

chitih svatantrā vishva siddhi hetuh [v.1]

Consciousness, of its own free will,
creates the universe out of itself.

It makes the One appear as many and the many as One. It turns the nondual into the dual, and the dual into the nondual.

From this Consciousness arise all the various powers: the yoga of yogis, the blissful realization of realized beings, the devotion of devotees, the poetry of poets, the wealth of the wealthy, the benevolence of those who follow dharma, the authority of kings, the courage of warriors, the austerity of those who do *tapasya*, the liberation of the liberated, and the destructive power of huge weapons. All these powers are part of that universal Consciousness. In the *Bhagavad Gītā* this power is called the glorious power of the Divine, the great power of yoga.

From this Consciousness arise endless miracles on both the inner and outer planes of existence. This conscious power is the

Sita of Lord Rama, the Radha of Lord Krishna, the Shakti of Lord Shiva, and the energy of the soul described in Vedanta. It is known by both names — Shiva as well as Shakti. Shiva and Shakti are different only in name; in reality, they are one and the same. Appearing as favorable or unfavorable, this energy manifests amazingly in an endless number of forms. In Shree Gurudev, too, there were innumerable miracles of this yogic power. This is the divine power of grace bestowed by a Siddha Guru on a disciple. And when it is bestowed on one who is ready, his experience of himself is different than before. Such a disciple has direct knowledge of these yogic truths: I am the Absolute. I am Shiva. I am That.

This power of Kundalini Shakti is situated in every human being at the base of the spine in the *mūlādhāra chakra* coiled three and a half times like a snake. This Shakti remains dormant until She is awakened. She has two aspects — outer and inner. When She turns outward, She provides the power for all the activities of the world. When She turns inward, spiritual practices become possible. She increases or decreases a seeker's glory depending on his past karma. She bestows all the capacities of worldly skills, from statesmanship to scientific research. With the help of Her outward-turning power, a person can do great work in any field. With the help of the inward power, yogis can attain omniscience, eloquence, the capacity for spiritual guidance, keen intelligence, and the ability to bestow grace and to guide its progress.

To awaken this dormant Kundalini Shakti is the work of the Guru. Until She is awakened, supreme happiness cannot be attained. The *Pratyabhijñāhridayam* says:

madhya vikāsāc chidānanda-lābhah / [v.17]

With the unfolding of the central channel,
supreme bliss is attained.

When the grace of the Guru awakens Kundalini, that great mystical power and the mother of yoga, then tremendous work begins within the disciple who is ready. If the process were written down in detail, it would make a very thick book, but to satisfy the reader who wants to know, here is a brief description.

When Kundalini is awakened, a new vitality spreads through

every pore of the body and a process of inner purification begins. In the beginning there may be overwhelming drowsiness, tremors, perspiration, sensations like electric shocks, tremendous heat, feelings of intense joy, spontaneous physical postures, and then a state of deep meditation like samadhi. The seeker may have the inner darshan of gods and goddesses, or of Siddhas. He may experience heaven or the realm of ancestors. He may see lights and hear inner music during meditation, or even during the waking state.

In the central channel of the subtle body, the *sushumnā nādī*, there are six *chakras*, ranging from the *mūlādhāra*, at the base of the spine, to the *sahasrāra*, at the crown of the head. When Kundalini awakens, the purification of these *chakras* begins. All the fluids of the body are rejuvenated. The incoming and outgoing breaths are equalized, and the breath is retained spontaneously. The knot of ignorance dissolves, and the illusion of separate individuality vanishes. All doubts are destroyed, and the union of the embodied soul and the Lord becomes real. Finally, the power of one's karmas weakens and disappears, and liberation in this very life is attained.

In a human body, the mind and *prāna* work closely together. When the mind is still, the *prāna* is still. When the mind and *prāna* are in equilibrium, everything functions harmoniously. When the reflection of the conscious Self falls upon this harmonized state, one is in a state of illumination even while going about one's worldly activities.

In this way, both the *prāna* and the mind are means of experiencing happiness and unhappiness, good and bad actions. The fruit of bad actions is unhappiness and the fruit of good actions is happiness. In the physical body, with the help of the mind and the *prāna*, the soul experiences the consequences of its previous actions. Only after the mind and *prāna* are peaceful, only then is it possible to experience complete bliss. After the awakening of Kundalini, after the incoming and outgoing breaths are equalized, then the mind becomes completely pure and one-pointed. A one-pointed mind brings the experience of samadhi. The experience of samadhi brings detachment. Then, very naturally, the mind is steady and free of thoughts. When this occurs, the transcendental state is attained. After that, the seeker experiences an all-pervasive state of pure bliss. He merges with this bliss and is completely fulfilled. This fulfillment is liberation. It is realization. It is enlightenment.

Enlightenment comes through the awakening of Kundalini, which is the great gift of the Guru's grace. The Guru's gift is immense, infinite, boundless. Only a disciple who is fully prepared, who is ripe, can understand this. With this gift from the Guru, the intellect forgets all sorrow and experiences steadfastness. With the grace of the Guru, the heart becomes full of love, and one experiences the nectar of bliss pervading the whole world. After receiving Shaktipat from the Guru, the intricacies of yoga become easy to understand, and then one can take rest in the bliss of Consciousness, which is beyond the realm of space. To such a compassionate Guru, a disciple is forever indebted.

The words of such a Guru are of the form of Vedic mantras, which are immortal. For a disciple, the words that shine forth from Shree Gurudev's heart are imperishable and divine. They can take you across the ocean of this world. The Guru's words come from the Self. On listening to them, this world becomes a paradise. The cycle of birth and death is destroyed, and the seeker is awakened from the nightmare of sorrow that arises from duality. The words of such a Guru are words of grace.

Many people assume that Bhagawan Nityananda never gave a mantra directly and that he never gave initiation. But this is not true. He did not belong exclusively to any individual, nor to any particular community or sect. Just as God does not belong to any country or individual, the same is true of saints and Gurus. Bhagawan Nityananda gave mantra initiation secretly to many devotees and seekers. To some he gave *Om*; to some *Ram*; to others *Namah Shivāya* or *So'ham*. Some seekers repeated their mantra secretly, while others boasted that Bhagawan had given a mantra exclusively to them. Those who received the mantra from Bhagawan and, understanding the greatness of the gift, kept it secret, did in the end attain something. Those who did not keep the mantra to themselves but made it public were unable to attain anything.

All the mantras Bhagawan Nityananda gave were filled with

his Shakti. He used to say, "Even though the mantras are different, the same conscious energy permeates them. The all-pervasive divine force is the same in all mantras and bears the same fruit."

Many people are grateful to Shree Gurudev. He gave many kinds of initiation. He gave the mantra and he taught *prānāyāma*. He has thousands of devotees. Some keep their devotion hidden and others are open about it.

CHAPTER SIX

The Great Liberation

Only one principle pervades the entire world.
It is indestructible and beyond decay.
That essential principle is our own inner Self.
It is neither near nor far because it is everywhere.
For Nityananda, neither the knowledge of the world
nor the world itself nor the body has any significance.
Nityananda is that principle who perceives the Self
in everything.

In this world, the ways of time are very strange. Its speed is unfathomable. Time has no compassion, no love, no forgiveness. Time knows only its own duty. It is said that time consumes even itself. When it does not spare its own self, what can be said about others? Time sees everyone as the same. It does not consider whether someone is a king or a young person or a child.

Time leapt toward Bhagawan Nityananda, toward that being whose darshan was a joy to the eyes, toward that one whose face brought happiness to endless numbers of devotees. Seeing him, an evil person experienced goodness, a bound soul felt liberated, a beggar felt rich, and someone devoid of good qualities had the experience of many virtues. Gurudev was the support of his devotees in this world that is so difficult to cross. And yet, he was slowly removed from our very eyes. What a cruel thing for time to do. But who can stop time?

Worldly people think of death as the end of life. So in the eyes of the world, Bhagawan Nityananda came to an end. But in reality, Shree Gurudev never left. He is eternal, immortal, without end. Even now he is sitting right there, just as he always did. How can *nityānanda*, eternal bliss, ever die? Just as the sun does not stop shedding light when it is invisible, similarly, Nityananda did not come to an end. Only an ignorant person thinks that the sun has disappeared or that Nityananda has died. Nityananda dwells within every creature. He permeates everything. The Upanishads say that the world was born from bliss, from *ānanda*. Nityananda is forever immortal.

If you truly wish to have his darshan, then search for him within yourself. Make your life full of detachment, renunciation, and love. Make your mind pure and do not look for faults in others. Then you yourself will become Nityananda.

But these are words for *jñānis*, for those who love knowledge. For his *bhaktas*, his loving devotees, that twelfth day of Ashadha in Samvat 2017, was extremely painful, anguished, and unendurable.

THE LAST DAY

Two months before, Shree Gurudev had started preparing for the great liberation. He had stopped eating. Sometimes he took water and occasionally a little fruit. He became quite thin. Even the pleas of his devotees could not persuade him to eat. They sent for the doctor. But Bhagawan was absorbed in his own bliss; he was not interested in doctors or medicines. He was his own master. No one could compel him to keep the body any longer.

Whether they belong to Brahma or an insect, bodies go through the same process. Birth, growth, change, illness, decay, and death:

these six stages apply to all bodies. This is nature's law, and it cannot be broken. In nature, what is finite can never be infinite. If this were not so, Rama and Krishna would still be with us in their physical form. Ever since it began, the universe has been bound by unchangeable laws. Whatever is born, one day will die. This is how it is.

No one imagined that Gurudev's physical body would come to an end so soon. On the day of Guru Purnima, he gave darshan lying down. On Sunday, August 6th, Gurudev sent for coffee to be given as *prasād* to everyone present. He smiled and gave Dr. Nicholson's little boy a piece of fruit. All the devotees were sitting, very quietly, as they always did. The regular visitors were standing at a distance. Two days later at 10:40 A.M. on Tuesday, August 8th, 1961, he passed away. His life ended in a large room on the upper floor of Shree Lakshmansha Khode's Bangalore House in Ganeshpuri. He was lying with his head toward the north. A few devotees were present: Boman Behram, Advocate D.M. Parulekar, Shree Chimanlal Parekh, Karianna Shetty, Babu Shetty, Shrimati Gangabai Shah, Kutiram Swami, Mahabal Swami, Dr. Nicholson, and others. Until the end, Shree Gurudev looked the same. He had the same radiance, peace, and serenity; nothing had changed.

A few minutes before the great liberation Shree Gurudev's hands and feet became straight. For several years his joints had been stiff from rheumatism. His destined suffering had come to an end. The scriptures say that great beings undergo their worldly suffering and then, leaving the body, attain nirvana.

Dr. Nicholson was gently rubbing Shree Gurudev's palms, and I was gently rubbing his feet. The flow of *prāna* left the feet. The doctor let go of his hands. The time of great liberation had come. The *prāna* was rising upward. I caught hold of Shree Gurudev's hands.

His face took on the same appearance that we had seen in the early days — the *shāmbhavī mudrā*, an outward gaze with an inward focus. He cast a loving look, full of grace, at the devotees on all sides, and then turned his eyes upward. The *sushumnā nādī* throbbed between his eyebrows. The sound of *Om*, beautiful and melodious, was heard, and his life-breath, his *prāna*, merged with the cosmic Consciousness.

I cried out "Gurudev!" and felt my head pulled down on his chest. Chimanlal Parekh put his hand on my back and said, "Muktananda Swami, is this your time to cry?"

I got up. It took a few moments for the devotees to realize what had happened. Before their eyes, Shree Gurudev had passed away. His body lay still and peaceful.

With his leaving, the world had lost the company of a great being, of a Siddha who was divine. He was a visible form of the formless Absolute. The departure of such a great being is very significant. When an ordinary human being dies, the soul leaves the body and, according to its karma, goes on to take another form. But in the case of great beings, who have realized their oneness with Brahman, with the highest Reality, with the all-pervasive Being, Consciousness, and Bliss (*sat chit ānanda*), the *prāna* does not travel to other planes; it does not leave the body.

The Upanishads say:

na tasya prāna utkramanti /

At the time of the final samadhi, the *prāna* does not leave; it merges in the *sahasrāra*.

Such a being is beyond any question of rebirth. His very presence uplifted seekers and destroyed their desires. There could be no question of his taking part in the cycle of rebirth, no question of his taking another body. So the *mahāsamādhi* of a great being is a unique occasion. Mantras are recited, *yajñas* performed, scriptures read, food distributed, and chanting offered — all to express the devotees' love and reverence and to remember him.

After Shree Gurudev left his body, the question arose of where he should be buried and how all the arrangements should be made. A committee was formed and I was made the head of it. The others on the committee were Shree Wadilal Chaturbhuja, Kakubhai Gokani, Laxam Khade, Chinmanlal Shah, Dr. Nicholson, Babubhai Gokani, Bhaskar Gandhi, Bango Patil, Kutiram Swami, Santaram Shetty, and P. K. Nair.

Darshan
for Thousands

When Shree Gurudev merged with his own inner Self, it was a serene and nectarean morning. For the lord of yogis, for a saint like Bhagawan Nityananda, there is no question of an auspicious hour for his last journey. He is beyond time and place. Whatever moment he chooses for his departure becomes auspicious. For him, north and south are equally holy. For one who is beyond auspicious and inauspicious, beyond sin and virtue, beyond all duality, everything relating to him is auspicious.

We placed Shree Gurudev's body facing north in the lotus posture on the armchair where he always sat. We decided to leave his body there for forty-eight hours so that the devotees could have his darshan. As he sat there, his face was lit with the same divine smile that we had seen during his life. Shree Gurudev's body did not deteriorate or lose its luster. That sacred body, which had been purified through yoga, underwent no change or decay at all. Many people felt the body was alive. Struck by the radiance and glow of the body, an eminent professor of Ayurveda, Shree Narayan Joshi, felt doubtful about its state and asked me if he could feel the pulse. But whatever had to happen had already happened.

As the news spread, crowds gathered for the last darshan of Shree Gurudev. Countless garlands were placed on his body. Chanting went on day and night. The people who came for his darshan were lost in deep sorrow and indescribable pain. Shree Gurudev was like God to them. In times of sorrow and danger, they would seek his help and always find comfort. They received happiness, peace, and satisfaction from him. Who would help them now? Who would understand their pain and sorrow and help them in hard times? The one who would lovingly ask them, "Have you been to the hot springs? Have you eaten? Have you had darshan?" — that one was gone forever. Everyone's heart was filled with sorrow. Even nature appeared sad and dejected. The sky was cloudy and the atmosphere heavy. There was no breeze; no air moved.

Everywhere, people spoke of Shree Gurudev. "Baba built a house and gave it to me." "I had no son and Baba gave me a son."

"He cured me of disease." "He gave me a shop." "He got a wife for my son." "He won my court case." Some said, "Shree Gurudev stilled my mind." Some said, "He showed me God; he made me a Siddha." They remembered all the good he had done for them and were filled with sorrow. "Now what will happen to us?" This thought disturbed them. Gurudev was, in fact, the support of their lives. Now they began to doubt their future.

These scenes continued for two days. Day and night, people kept arriving. Buses ran nonstop from Vasai. People from nearby villages walked for miles to have their last darshan. The hotels and restaurants ran out of food. Accommodations overflowed; people had to camp beside the road and in the fields. It was as if the Prayag *kumbha mela* were being held in Ganeshpuri. There was a sea of human heads in all directions.

Finally, Thursday came. Very early in the morning, during *brahmamūhurta*, with the auspicious chanting of *Om*, Shree Gurudev's body was given a ritual bath by some devotees and disciples, including Kutiram Swami, Jananand Swami, and Mahabal Swami. At 7:30 his body was placed in a jeep bedecked with flowers. His last journey began with the chant *Om Namo Bhagavate Nityānandāya*, accompanied by drums and other instruments. Between three and four hundred thousand people wept as they had one last glimpse of their Gurudev. They poured flowers on him unceasingly. The road was washed with the tears of the mourners and with showers of rain. The funeral procession made a circle around Kailas Nivas and then reached Vaikuntha, Bhagawan Nityananda's original home in Ganeshpuri. Shree Gurudev's body was brought near the burial place. The ritual consecration of the ground was performed by Shree Wadilal Chaturbhuja Gandhi. As Vedic mantras were recited, Shree Gurudev's body was lowered onto a deerskin seat and surrounded by camphor, sandalwood, sacred oils, gold, and jewels. Then, as people watched, he disappeared into the earth.

On this site a large temple was built with a beautiful statue of Shree Gurudev. It has become a place of pilgrimage for many devotees.

HIS ONGOING PRESENCE

*I*n this way, after having lived in Ganeshpuri for twenty-five to thirty years, and having worked to uplift humanity, he simply folded up his *līlā*, his divine play, and merged into the Self. Without his presence Ganeshpuri began to seem lifeless. The devotees thought Bhagawan had left them and gone. But where could he go? He was always here, he is here, and he will always remain here. To think he is no longer here is illusion, ignorance. He is present in every object, animate and inanimate, in every particle of nature. Where is that place that is without his presence? There is no question of his having left. But it is true that we can no longer have the darshan of his very beautiful form.

Shree Gurudev is as he was. He is here. He was perfect and will remain perfect from the beginning of time to the end. He was beyond time. How could he be bound by time? He has not gone anywhere. He gives this assurance himself. Many people have his darshan in different places. He appears in dreams and gives guidance. Thousands of people come to Ganeshpuri and their wishes are fulfilled. Day and night people sing of his greatness and glory. Such unwavering faith and devotion are amazing and are rarely seen elsewhere. It is hard to imagine someone coming to Ganeshpuri and being unaffected by the grace and greatness of Bhagawan Nityanandaji. The entire atmosphere there reverberates with his name and greatness. There is a verse in Narada's *Bhakti Sūtras*:

tirthi-kurvanti tirthani / [v. 69]

Saints enhance the sanctity of holy places.

Shree Gurudev made this verse come alive in Ganeshpuri. His original hut, Vaikuntha, is now his simple but majestic Samadhi Shrine. Here the devotees do puja and *āratī* three times a day. Some recite the *Rudram* and other hymns; others perform worship of various kinds. Some sing devotional songs according to their faith and go home feeling fortunate. Some see him during their meditation in the form of light and are thrilled and happy to have this darshan. Some say they received a command from him to recite the *Gītā*. In this way, the devotees continue in the knowledge of Shree Gurudev's greatness. There is not a shred of doubt that Shree Gurudev is present now. I say with certainty that even now he is here in that same form and even speaks in the same way.

Shree Gurudev's mission did not end with his body. It is even stronger now and continues to increase steadily. His influence is ongoing and will never end. It is not limited by space and time. Every day, people visit his Samadhi Shrine and have their wishes fulfilled. Many more devotees come to Ganeshpuri than ever before. Just as Shree Gurudev enhanced Ganeshpuri as a center of pilgrimage, the same work is expanding today.

Everything is going well because of Shree Gurudev's grace. There is electricity in Ganeshpuri, so it attracts more visitors. The state government has built a holiday camp; a high school and hospital are being built. Surrounded by natural beauty, Ganeshpuri is heaven on earth. Here, natural beauty and spirituality will flow together forever. For seekers, such a place is very rare. Here they attain their goal.

Therefore, I can say that Shree Gurudev is here. His presence is immortal, full of Consciousness, and all pervasive.

What is needed to see Shree Gurudev is only inner vision.

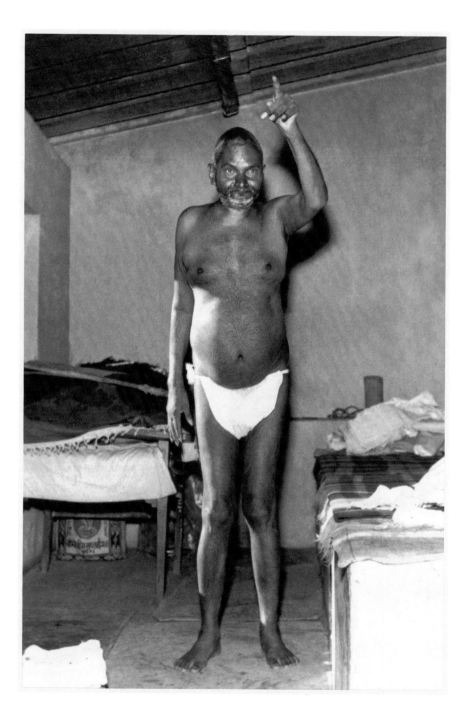

CHAPTER SEVEN

His Teachings

Without a Sadguru, no one can cross this world.
Until you receive wisdom,
you can never be free of sorrow.
When the Sadguru shows the way,
only then do sorrows come to an end.
When he imparts teachings,
only then does the mind become tranquil.

Shree Gurudev's influence and presence were, in themselves, so powerful that he did not need to give lectures or teach
explicitly. Even so, the devotees always hoped for a few words from
him; they were eager to know how he would answer their questions. For their sake, Gurudev would occasionally speak a little. He
emphasized purity of mind, purity of feeling, and faith in God.
These three phrases, uttered in his sacred speech, cover the range
of his teaching and contain the essence of all scriptures as well. A
person who regards these teachings as a mantra from the Guru and
follows them will certainly attain happiness in this world and
become worthy of the Guru's grace.

PURITY OF MIND

The ancient seers have said that the primary cause of happiness and sorrow, virtue and sin, heaven and hell is the mind. The one who makes his mind as pure as gold is practicing the highest action. The perennial philosophy of the Indian tradition is contained in the four Vedas, the eighteen Puranas, the twenty-one Agamas, the thirty-two Smritis, the *Rāmāyana* and the *Mahābhārata*, as well as other scriptures. They all maintain that good actions purify the mind, that a pure mind leads to the knowledge of God, and that through this divine knowledge, one attains liberation.

For a human being, the mind has fundamental importance. The mind determines a person's birth and also his actions. Bhagawan Nityananda used to say, "When the mind is there, a person is an ordinary human being. When the mind has been transcended, a person becomes a great being, a saint."

The poet Sundardas says:

mana miti jai eka brahma nija saro hai /

When the mind is still, the one Supreme Being
is seen as the Self.

The person whose mind is tranquil and without malice enjoys good health. His reason is not disturbed by desire for sense pleasures. He is free of unhappiness, free of sorrow, free of fear. He moves through this world fearlessly.

The mind can lead a person along two completely different roads. An impure mind takes one along impure pathways, into bad company, impure actions and thoughts, and eventually to hell. A pure mind with good thoughts leads one along the path of virtue, into good company, righteous action, and ultimately to liberation.

Shree Gurudev used to say, "God is the witness of your mind." The experience of God takes place in a pure mind. For the sake of this experience, keep the mind completely pure.

In the *Bhagavad Gītā*, the Lord, explaining His functions, says:

indriyānām manash-chasmi [10:22]

Among the instruments of perception and action,
I am the mind.

The one who appears as the witness of the mind, that Consciousness is God. Knowing this, how should one care for the mind?

> *O mind, drop this restlessness and shed your cleverness;*
> *cast off all impurities and do not fall into negativities,*
> *such as malice.*
> *You have plunged your mind in impurities.*
> *Wake up now.*
> *The mind is the root of old age and death.*
> *Chant the name of Nityananda.*
> *This foolish mind imagines that worldly pleasures*
> *are the only bestower of good and bad fortune.*
> *The mind leads you to disastrous acts*
> *by creating thoughts of attaining this or rejecting that.*
> *When the mind becomes purified*
> *by chanting the name of the Guru,*
> *then Consciousness shines forth and bestows on you*
> *the state of Muktananda.*

Make the mind free of expectation of all worldly pleasures. Make the mind like the Guru, like Nityananda. With concentration, pray to the Guru and worship him. Through this worship, the mind will become pure. As soon as the mind becomes pure, the world will appear as the form of the Self, and love will arise for all creatures. You will realize: Shree Nityananda is in me, and I am in Nityananda!

This experience is the fruit of austerities. It is liberation itself, and it comes through God's grace.

PURITY OF FEELING

The second aspect of Shree Gurudev's instruction is purity of feeling, which means equality of vision and innocence of heart. A person is shaped by his feelings. From impure attitudes come anger, hatred, ignorance, infatuation, laziness, and carelessness.

Then a person begins to enjoy cheating others, insulting them, and causing pain. He gets carried away by *rajas*, and greed increases. As *rajas* grows, the craving for sense pleasures becomes stronger. Such a person will even commit sins to gratify his selfish appetites. His impure feelings blind him so that he cannot perceive the eternal Lord, who pervades this world. Thus he sinks lower and lower, and his life becomes one of sheer misery. That is why Shree Gurudev always tells us to cultivate purity of feeling.

O my dear ones! Take Shree Gurudev's teaching to heart. Purify your feelings. Through pure feeling, God can be seen everywhere. Through pure feeling, a person becomes divine, and others are drawn to follow his example.

> *Seek refuge in pure thoughts; discard impure thoughts.*
> *Knowing Brahman through purity of heart,*
> *worship That constantly.*
> *With purity in your heart, attain the realization of your Self.*
> *Repeat the name of the Sadguru;*
> *remember God with the highest wisdom in your heart,*
> *and thus you will achieve immortality and indestructibility.*
> *If you entertain impure thoughts,*
> *you experience the tortures of hell.*
> *There are countless negativities —*
> *sorrow, delusion, pride, greed —*
> *that make you suffer in this world.*
> *Ignoring the liberating lotus feet of Nityananda,*
> *you choose to be trapped by the snares of this world.*
> *Muktananda says that purity of heart is the essence*
> *of Nityananda's teachings.*

FAITH IN GOD

Shree Gurudev's third teaching is faith in God. The *Bhagavad Gītā* says:

shraddhāvāṅl labhate jñānam [4:39]

One who possesses faith attains knowledge.

The essence of faith is to believe that the unseen is as real as the seen. Faith is the root of all dharmas, all religions. To have complete faith in the feet of the Lord is the first and foremost way of attaining devotion. Every day with faith we should sing the praises of God, contemplating His qualities, His acts, and His beautiful names. In this way, our devotion will become strong. By singing His attributes, they will permeate our minds. By contemplating Him and following Him, love will arise in our hearts, and we will cross the ocean of worldliness.

Faith creates amazing miracles. Faith makes the earth move; faith makes a weak person strong; faith makes possible the impossible. Faith does not argue or debate with any one. Without faith, life is as dry as a dessert without sweetness. Faith is the magnet to attract God's grace. Faith is the root of victory. Faith attains the unattainable. Faith makes it possible to experience Nityananda in the heart. Faith in God turns poison into nectar. Therefore, Shree Gurudev used to say, "Have faith, have faith!"

With faith, a person can cross any kind of difficulty. Without faith, he drowns in the ocean of worldliness. Living without faith is a form of death. The *Bhagavad Gītā* says that lack of faith, cynicism, leads to an endless cycle of birth and death:

ashraddadhānāh purusha dharmasyāya paramtapa /
aprāpya mām nivartante mrityusamsāravartmani // [9:3]

Those who have no faith in this knowledge, Arjuna, do not attain Me and are born again on the path of death and transmigration.

Therefore, have faith. You will be able to see the Guru manifesting in your own Self. It is faith that makes fruitful the mantra, the deity, and *prasād*. And on the same topic the *Bhagavad Gītā* says,

shraddhāmayo 'yam purusho [17:3]

Faith constitutes the very essence of a human being.

MEDITATION

Shree Gurudev used to tell seekers to meditate. When people asked questions about sadhana, or spiritual practice, he would say, "Why talk so much! Meditate! You will get everything through meditation." The Upanishads and other scriptures have said that God dwells in the heart. So why not seek for God within yourself? Why wander from one place to another? Why practice austerities without seeking the One in the heart? A poet has written, "Where do you look for me, O seeker? I am with you; I cannot be found in a temple or a mosque, in Kashi or on Mount Kailas."

The *Bhagavad Gītā* says:

dhyānenātmani pashyanti kechid ātmānam ātmanā / [13:25]

Some perceive the Self within through meditation.

The Self is the subtlest of the subtle; even so, it can be seen through meditation.

This very world is a form of meditation, and a person perceives the world according to his feeling. Our understanding of other people, of the world, and of God Himself is determined by our attitude and feeling.

A person becomes what he meditates on. Shree Ramakrishna Paramahamsa used to have the feeling that he was Hanuman as he prayed to Lord Rama, and during that period of his life he actually resembled Hanuman.

Through meditation, one becomes that on which his mind dwells. That is, whatever the seeker meditates on, that is what he becomes. This is how an insect turns into a bee. The bee encloses the insect in a house of mud and then keeps poking at it from all sides. The insect is so terrified of the bee that it constantly keeps thinking of the bee. The result is that it becomes the bee.

In the *Aparokshānubhūti*, it is said:

bhavitam tivra-vegena yad-vas-tu nischayatmana /
pumams-taddhi bhavec-chighram jneyam bhramara-kitavat //
[v. 140]

One becomes exactly what one's mind dwells on intensely and with firm resolve. This can be understood through the analogy of an insect turning into a bee.

When this is the case, what is so improbable about becoming God through meditation on Him? In just the same way, one becomes like the Guru through contemplation of him.

Meditation means to still the thought-waves of the mind completely. Stabilizing the mind is the goal of meditation. All the sorrows of the world are due to the fluctuations of the mind. Ecstasy lies in the thought-free state of mind. But making the mind free of thoughts is not so easy. The mind always wants to lean on one thought or another. Therefore, to become established in the Self it is necessary to have an external support for a while.

A person transcends thought by means of thought. In the *Yoga Sūtras* there is an aphorism of Patanjali that says:

vīta-rāga-vishayam vā chittam / [1:37]

Focus the mind on one who is free from attachment.

A perfected saint is such a being. By seeking the shelter of such beings, the desires of many lifetimes are destroyed. Dispassion develops, and the bliss of the Self arises in the heart. Therefore keep remembering Shree Nityanandaji. You will experience eternal bliss, *nityānanda*, pulsating within.

KNOWLEDGE

*A*long with the command to meditate, Bhagawan Nityananda also emphasized the importance of knowledge. He was a great lover of Vedanta, and he manifested nondual consciousness fully. Vedanta had become a dynamic force in him. His nondual awareness could be seen in his actions. Shree Gurudev used to say that pervading everything is blissful Consciousness. In everything, whether animate or inanimate, God exists. In the form of the inner Self, He dwells in a human body. He is the one who has become the light of the eyes and illumines everything. He makes the arms and legs move. He gives the ears the power to hear. He moves the *prāna* throughout the body. He makes all the senses active. That same Lord pervades the entire world completely, never losing His oneness.

Shree Gurudev urged seekers to penetrate the apparent differences of this world through meditation and knowledge, to reach the underlying Reality and have the darshan of the Lord both inside and outside.

You will find your own Self in the form of the Lord. Recognize your true nature: you are that transcendent Being. You are that supreme Nityananda, through whose play you can experience bliss in this world.

PART TWO

He Opened the Gates of Heaven for Me

CHAPTER EIGHT

The Simple Truth Straight Away

Siddhas have their own independent plane of existence called Siddhaloka. It is a very beautiful world. The Siddhas who live there have a different perception of time than we do in this world. A thousand of our years is like a second for them. There is no day or night there. That world is illuminated by its own light; it doesn't need the sun or the moon. Just as we have the blue light of Consciousness shimmering within us, that same blue light is shimmering and scintillating in Siddhaloka.

From time to time beings from Siddhaloka come here to perform some work. Great beings like Jnaneshwar, Shirdi Sai Baba, Zipruanna, and my Baba Nityananda all came from that place. They come to our world because they are directed to do so. They sow seeds, and after a while they leave. When the seed sprouts, it grows into a plant; then it becomes a tree with many branches. Eventually it bears a lot of fruit and becomes something great.

There are many planes of existence. Just as the world of the moon exists, just as heaven exists, which is called Indraloka, in the same way, Siddhaloka exists, the world of the Siddhas. Nityananda was a being who came from that world. He was an ancient Siddha. Since the beginning of creation, there have been many Siddhas, and he is one of them.

Nityananda was a great Siddha yogi. When he was born, he was a Siddha. Even though he was a self-born Siddha, still he had to have a Guru. Even Lord Krishna had a Guru called Sandipani. It is the spiritual law — one has to have a Guru. And Lord Rama, who was also an incarnation of God, had a Guru called Vasishtha.

My Guru also had a Guru. His name was Ishwara Iyer. My Baba stayed in his house and he would wash the dishes and sweep the floor. Ishwara Iyer was a great yogi who had practiced austerities. He was an enlightened Siddha Guru who had received the highest blessings through the compassion of the Sun God, the illuminer of all three worlds. The one who loved him above all was Nityananda.

When my Baba was very young, his Guru left his body. In India the bodies of Hindus are always cremated; they don't bury their dead. So when his dead body was cremated, my Guru left that place, wearing just his loincloth, and sometimes not even that. Later, he began to wear more clothes, just for the sake of other people.

When my Baba was very young, he would automatically perform extraordinary miracles, but when he grew up, he left all that. He was an omniscient being; still he appeared as if he didn't know much. He was a great knower of the scriptures; still he appeared as if he hadn't learned anything. In his younger days some people thought he was mad, or that he was affected by a devil or by a ghost. The scriptures say that the state of a Siddha and the state of ordinary people are as different as owls and crows. What is daytime for a crow is night for an owl, and what is daytime for an owl is night for a crow.

Great beings appear to be different from each other on the outside. One may be inert, one like a ghost, and one may seem intoxicated. But all of them are lost in the love of God. Nityananda Baba was very intoxicated all the time. His eyes were filled with that intoxication, and his body too. When one experiences the supreme nectar of a great being, compared to that, everything else becomes meaningless, tasteless. Inside and outside, he is filled with the intoxication of devotion. He becomes immersed in it. Wherever he looks, God is standing there. Notions of mine and thine disappear. Everything is God. The state of these great beings is marvelous. There was Rang Avadhut and Zipruanna and Hari Giri Baba and Sai Baba. And there was Nityananda Baba. However different they appear, they are all lost in the love of God.

My Guru was such a great ecstatic being that he had lost himself within himself. He lost himself — not in a jungle — but in God. He lost himself — not in a party or a religion or a caste system — but in God. If you lose yourself in That, then you attain your own Self.

If a person makes mistakes or creates problems, people talk and write about him. Nityananda didn't do anything historical, anything that would be in the newspapers. He lost himself completely in God and he attained his own Self.

For him, all religions were equal. For him, all mantras and all people were equal. He would sit in a public place. People could meet him; no one had to have an appointment.

When people asked him, "Will you show God to us?" he would say, "Yes, He is within you. Go there." This was his great teaching. The supreme Truth dwells right within you. Whoever saw God saw God right within himself.

Nityananda had thousands and thousands of disciples who received his energy. He didn't use ostentatious rituals to give initiation. He would make a gesture toward someone, and that person would receive his grace. He would utter a single word to someone, and that person would receive grace. Whatever a Siddha says, that is the mantra. Whatever a Siddha does, that is yoga. Whatever a Siddha speaks, that is knowledge.

Such great beings don't come into this world to have two or three disciples or to be someone's trademark. Such beings come into this world to fulfill Lord Krishna's promise in the *Bhagavad Gītā*: "Whenever there is a decline of righteousness, whenever people engage themselves in worldly matters, whenever people turn away from going inside themselves, O Arjuna, then I take birth in this world."

There is a powerful tradition of Gurus called the Siddha Yoga tradition, in which the Master can touch a disciple or just point a finger at him, and thereby set in motion the process of Siddha Yoga. There are plenty of gurus who can teach *japa*, discipline, *prāṇāyāma*, and *āsanas* — these are ordinary things. But with the grace and blessing of a Siddha Guru we don't have to do yoga; it happens spontaneously within us. We call the yoga that happens like this by itself Siddha Yoga, and mantra yoga, *raja yoga*, hatha yoga, *laya yoga*, *bhakti yoga* — all yogas are part of it. A man can sow a tiny seed and it will grow into an enormous tree that will blossom and bear fruit; a Guru like this is very rare. It takes a lot of courage to make friends with a Siddha and spend your time with him.

There was a great exponent of Siddha Yoga in the tradition of the Siddhas — my Guru. People would get Shaktipat by just coming into his presence. In one of the scriptures there is a dialogue between Shiva and Shakti, in which Shiva says that there are many gurus who take money and service from their disciples, but rare is the Guru who will take his disciple's mind and not his money, who will steal the mind that is tormenting him.

Some Gurus will tell you the simple truth straight away. Baba Nityananda was like that. As soon as a seeker came to him, my Baba would say, "Why are you wandering? All is within. Go and sit at home. What is there outside?"

He was not the kind of guru who would say, "First you must serve me for twelve years; you must make this offering and then you will receive something." He would always say, "Why are you wandering here and there? Everything is within. Go and sit at home."

THE HEART IS THE HUB

If someone were to ask me what gives meaning to my life, I could only say, "The name of my Guru." I discovered everything within me by my Guru's grace. Bhagawan Shree Nityananda was a perfect Guru. His essential teaching was: "The heart is the hub of all sacred places. Go there and roam." By remembering and worshiping such a Master, one becomes holy.

I met my Guru when I was very young. I was almost sixteen and still in school. I was rather bored with my studies, but I was very active in play. I was very good at playing. Gurudev loved children, so whenever he came to our school all of us would leave our classes and follow him. The moment we followed him, he would start running and shouting. We would run after him, and then he would climb up a tree and sit on a branch. We would just stay there under the tree. He was a great runner, he had great speed. He was a great walker too, he walked very fast. He walked in a strange way, in the state of an *avadhūt*.

Whenever he came to my school, the teachers would be very upset, but the children would follow him anyway. He would go into a candy store, reach into the containers, throw candy to the children, and then take off again. Still, the shopkeepers never complained, because whenever he gave away their candy, their sales went up.

So when he came to my school, I began to follow him too. I had this feeling that I wanted to become like him, that such a thing would be much better than anything else.

In those days he didn't stay in one place for very long. He kept walking and walking, day and night. He would walk forty miles a day, and then he would disappear. He wore just a loincloth, and he would walk and walk. Finally he went to Ganeshpuri where he settled permanently.

After I met him, I gave up school. I also started traveling. First I went to Karnataka where I began to study scriptures, and where I met a great Siddha called Siddharudha Swami. I continued to travel all over India, and I met two other great saints: one in Ahmedabad, who was called Jaganath Baba, and another one in Dwarka called Shree Ram Baba, who used to repeat *Shree Ram, Shree Ram* all the time. He lived on the beach and he was an ecstatic being. When I met them, I thought I was smarter than they were, so I couldn't attain anything even from them.

I also used to go to Ganeshpuri and meet my Baba quite often. He wouldn't keep anyone close to him right away. I would go and stay with him for a few days. Then he would tell me to go and travel some more. So I would leave and travel some more. But then I would miss him and go back to see him again. After a while I would become restless and leave again. For about fifteen years I kept coming and going from my Baba's place. Sometimes he would tell me where to go and it would be a place far away from him.

I didn't spare any of the holy places in India. I didn't spare any of the great temples. I didn't spare any of the great beings. I searched intensely for God in caves, mountains, and forests. I do not remember in exactly how many temples I sought Him or in how many shrines I meditated on Him to no avail. I prayed in so many different temples, but only hours slipped by and I was still without peace. I practiced severe austerities, but they only emaciated my body without taking me closer to God. I practiced *prānāyāma* and struggled with other hatha yoga techniques for a prolonged period, but I only became proud that I was a good yogi; I did not obtain peace. I constantly repeated the divine Name. I sang devotional songs, even with professional singers, until I was weary. I told beads, put the sacred mark on my forehead, and let my hair grow into matted locks. But all that I had were the beads, the sacred mark, and the long locks. Time passed without any real gain.

Then I set out in search of a guide. One naked one turned out to be addicted to the pipe, while another asked me to pierce my ears in the Shaivite manner. One told me to smear my body with sacred ash, another to wear a black garment. Yet another suggested saffron robes. One instructed me to observe silence. Thus, my search continued until I was exhausted. Then I wandered all by myself, pondering the mysteries of life. In the course of those wanderings, I ran into an unusual, naked saint named Zipruanna. He was very great. Although he appeared to be a fool to worldly-minded fools, he was omniscient. He seemed a naked mendicant only to those who were spiritually naked, being without knowledge. However, he was the owner of a vast treasure of wisdom — a true millionaire. I loved him at first sight. We became friends. What a combination! One was a naked fakir while the other was a well-dressed, modern renunciant. He said, "O you crazy one, God is within! Why do you seek Him outside?"

I said, "Instruct me."

"That is not for me to do," he replied. "Go back to Ganeshpuri and stay there. Your treasure lies there. Go and claim it."

So I went back to Ganeshpuri once again and met Nityananda Baba, the supreme *avadhūt*. I was overjoyed. No — I was fulfilled. After a bath in the hot springs, I went for his darshan. He was poised in a simple, easy posture on a plain cot, smiling gently. His eyes were open but his gaze was directed within. What divine luster glowed in those eyes! His body was dark, and he was wearing a simple loincloth. He said, "So you've come."

"Yes, Sir," I answered. I stood for a while and then sat down. There I realized the highest. I am still sitting there.[*]

HIS OPEN HANDS

𝒯t is very difficult to talk about Nityananda. His behavior, his manner, and his discipline were different from our understanding. He was a great and unique being. First of all, he was free from company. Even his fingers were always completely straight; he never folded them. It shows that when he gave up something, he gave it up completely. He never got attached to it again. Even though his fingers were very stiff, sometimes he would pick up leaves and rubbish and throw them away.

Only occasionally would he speak; however, you could not understand him. He was such an extraordinary being that he knew the past, the present, and the future; still, he remained as though he knew nothing.

If anyone went to him becoming very small, becoming very humble, then he would also act humble and talk and give instructions to that person. If anyone went to him acting like a great scholar, a learned person, a rich person, or a person who had power, then he would close his eyes, turn inside, and become very quiet. He had equal vision. He did not consider anyone inferior, low, or ignorant. He did not consider anyone pure, great, or very smart either. He did not see good or bad.

---

[*]This account, based on original transcripts, is more detailed than the one in *Light on the Path*. During Baba's wandering years, he visited many great beings, including Bhagawan Nityananda, but he did not yet recognize him as his Guru. Finally, when the time was right, Zipruanna sent him back to Ganeshpuri. This time Baba realized that Bhagawan Nityananda was indeed his Guru, and he settled down to do his sadhana with him.

For him, spirituality and worldly life were one and the same. If people asked him mundane questions about life, he would answer those questions. He never felt that one had to be a seeker, that one should ask questions only from the scriptures or about knowledge.

He never liked to sit for a long time. He loved to walk around. Even at night, he would walk around. While walking he would keep his head down and he kept his eyes closed too — that is how he walked. He either looked down or he looked up. He never looked straight out. He was always in an intoxicated state. It was his way of life to get up at three o'clock and take a bath in the hot springs. In the daytime he would remain absorbed in his own Self. At night he would talk to his devotees. I never saw him sleeping at night nor did I ever see him get tired. I never felt that he wanted to sleep. He had very simple food — just *dāl* and vegetables, a little rice, and sometimes coffee. He used to sit on a very simple and plain bench. His bed was also very simple; at the end, he was sleeping only on a thin mattress.

People used to bring him a lot of things. He never took any interest in them. However, the people around him made good use of them. Every great being has his own ways. If anyone visited my Baba and gave him money, he would say, "Dust, dust! Throw it away!" He wouldn't touch the money. There would be heaps of money in front of him, and it was put to good use, but he never touched it.

Even though many, many people went to see him, they would all become very quiet in his presence. As people kept watching him, they would feel him inside themselves and they would feel knowledge rising within. There was no need to take courses.

Even though his eyes were open, he never looked at other people — that's not what he liked. He always liked to gaze inside and become absorbed in his own inner Self. His eyes were always half open. He had a big belly because of long, inner retention of the breath, called *kumbhaka*. His body was completely dark, black. He wore only a loincloth. He was so handsome that not only young people and adults, but even old people kept watching and watching him.

Without talking, he gave instructions. Without giving the

touch, he awakened the inner Shakti. He didn't have to hold question-and-answer sessions. Without having to answer them, he did answer people's questions. It is very difficult to talk about such an extraordinary being. Also, it is difficult to understand his language.

He was very intoxicated all the time. His eyes were filled with intoxication. His body was filled with intoxication. If he was lying down it would take him two hours to turn to the other side. He wasn't like me; I am so active. Rang Avadhut's state was something different, Zipruanna's state was something different, Hari Giri Baba's state was something different, Sai Baba's state was something different. And Nityananda Baba's state was something unique.

***

*J*ust as a river that has merged in the ocean becomes the ocean, in the same way a being who has merged in God, who has become God, who lives as God, such a being is called the Guru. Even though he has this human form, still the divine energy, the Shakti, lives within him, blazing in its light. When people used to watch my Baba, they would receive Shaktipat just like that. They didn't have to receive the mantra from him. Just by watching him, changes would begin to take place in them. If he threw an object at a person, say a banana, and that person ate the banana, he would receive Shaktipat. My Baba didn't need to have formal initiation or rituals or ceremonies. This is the characteristic of a Siddha.

All kinds of people came to him, not only devotees. People came who wanted the name of the winning horse in the next day's horse race. Gamblers came wanting a tip. All these people would gather around my Baba and wait. No matter how much they were asked to leave, they wouldn't. Real seekers go to a great being such as my Baba to receive the supreme Shakti, but all those people wanted was the name of the winning horse.

In the beginning he would tell them very politely, "All right, now it's time to go." But they wouldn't leave. So he would pick up anything he could get his hands on — sticks or stones — and throw them at the people. He didn't use abusive terms as much as I do, but sometimes he did. He would say, "You father of a monkey, get out of here." Even from those blows, people received Shaktipat. All their bad habits and difficulties would start to disappear.

Such beings are called supreme Siddhas. However they behave, their actions bestow only grace. If they mind their manners and say very politely, "Oh, please come here," that is grace. If they say, "You unworthy wretch, get out of here," that is also grace. Good manners are for other people. This is how Gurus are. There was Shaktipat in his abusive terms; there was Shaktipat in his sticks.

There was a time when people in Ganeshpuri asked me where Muktananda Swami was, how he lived, and how he spent his days. I would conceal myself to that extent. I would not even wear saffron clothes while going to Ganeshpuri. I would roll up my saffron clothes in a bundle and go to Ganeshpuri incognito so that I would not be noticed by people there. The more anonymous I stayed in those days, the more famous I seem to be becoming now.

I led my life around my Guru, Nityananda, without showing off my knowledge. I behaved as though I were a great fool. I never let anyone know about all that I had received. Even though I went there I wouldn't sit too close to him. I would sit far away but where I could still see him. I learned everything from what he was teaching other people, what he was telling other people.

I wouldn't speak to anyone; I wouldn't make friends with anyone. Some people used to say I had a lot of pride and some people that I was a great fool. In this way, I received two kinds of degrees. I lived with those two degrees in Gurudev's ashram. This is absolutely true and this is the way one should live.

AUGUST 15, 1947

My Guru was a great aid in crushing my ego. I was a kind of half scholar; I had read some books here and there, and I had some broken knowledge. If you only study a little bit here and there, it's not good. Also I had changed my clothes; I had put on the robes of a swami. Because I was playing a role, I couldn't sit still. I played my role by jumping here and there. My Baba must have undergone a lot of suffering in trying to stake me out. But he did. Finally, after a long time, he gave me Shaktipat.

For a long time India was under the control of England. However, on August 15, 1947, it became liberated. Just as India was a slave of another power, in the same way I was a slave of my own senses; I was under their control. On the very same day that Lord Mountbatten said, "India has become free," my Sadguru, my Gurudev, told me that I had also become free.

On this day sometime between eight and nine in the morning, my Gurudev offered me *pādukās*, his sandals. In those days I used to live in Vajreshwari. (Where the ashram is now there were three rooms that were closed up; they weren't being used.) I would visit my Gurudev at his ashram every day. Usually I stood far away from him, but today I went very close to him. He was wearing these *pādukās*, walking back and forth; then he came and stood right before me. He came very, very close to me, and I began to sweat. I closed my eyes. He stood in front of me for a long time, thinking that I would open my eyes. Then he said, "Hey!" and I opened my eyes.

"Put these *pādukās* on," he said. I replied, "You have worn these *pādukās*. How can I wear them?" He laughed, and I said, "If you really want to give them to me, I will stretch my shawl out and you can place them in the shawl."

Then he lifted one foot at a time and placed the *pādukās* in the shawl. I became extremely happy. I put them on my head, and as I did this, I almost lost consciousness. He was still standing right in front of me. I was facing south and he was facing north. He was muttering and then he went inside. I was standing there with the *pādukās* on my head, and when he went inside I left to go back to Vajreshwari.

I walked down the road, only half-conscious, until I reached the *audumbara* tree, which you see when you walk down there. After that I don't know what happened. I don't know how I walked to the little temple of the *devī*, where the present ashram is, but I did, and I sat down in front of it for a long time, for hours on end. Maybe I sat there so long since it was the place where I was supposed to be. I'm still sitting here. I carried those *pādukās* and sat down in this place. Until the end of time I am going to be sitting right here.

My Baba's cook had made *bhajiyās*, delicious fried plantains, and Baba had brought out a tray of them and asked, "Where is he? Where is he?" But I had left. So he saved the *bhajiyās* just like that on the tray. I went to him the next evening and he gave me those *bhajiyās*. I ate them until my stomach was really full. Then he said, "There are three rooms. Go and sit there." The three rooms were right here in what is now the ashram. So I came and sat down here.

After I went and sat there, I didn't ask my Guru, "What should I do here? What should I eat?" There was no question of asking what I should eat or drink. Nityananda Baba received so many things. Some people used to bring bread from Bombay, and I used to eat that dry bread.

I visited Nityananda Baba every day. One day he told me, "Now leave this place and go to Suki, to a place where you will find only fields." I went to that place and sat in the fields at Suki.

It took me nine years to complete my sadhana. The moment my Guru bestowed Shaktipat, I received Shakti; but to become like Shakti takes a long time.

THE WORD
BECAME WILDFIRE

My Guru, in his supreme compassion, transmitted a holy word to me, and that word banished all darkness from within me. When the sun rises, all the darkness disappears from the world. You don't have to ask it to go; the moment the sun comes up it goes away by itself. The darkness in me was banished in the same way by the word my Guru gave me.

That Siddha gave me one word that completely transformed me, but I had to spend such a long time with him to receive it. The word I received after so many years spread through my body from head to toe like wildfire carried by the wind. It produced in me both inner heat and the coolness of joy.

Before meeting my Guru, I had practiced many different kinds of yoga, but it was I who had practiced them. However, that word activated a spontaneous yoga within me. I was filled with amazement. What postures, *mudrās*, and breathing processes! Everything happened on its own. After attaining divine realization, I understood my compassionate Guru.

After the awakening of the Shakti, this process of yogic movements began to take place within my entire body. What power that word had! I almost hesitate to write all of this. It revealed whatever was within me — in my heart and in my head. I saw my own double many times. In the *sahasrāra* at the crown of the head, I perceived the brilliance of a thousand suns. I also saw the Blue Being. Sometimes I would lose myself within; then I would regain consciousness. It was like a play, similar to that of the waking and dream states. Even now, I do not know where I lose my small self and from where it returns. It is so amusing — I lose myself, then find myself. I have seen the center of true joy; there I lose myself and from there I return. I am ecstatic! I have found the best place of all, right within myself.

I have rediscovered that which I never lost. Still, my addiction has not left me. *Jai Gurudev!* Such a great addiction to the Guru! *Guru Om!* The repetition of this great mantra occurs even in my dreams. I do not know who repeats it there. My Guru's picture seems to come alive for me. When I look at his eyes, I see radiance. When I gaze at his body, it seems to be moving. When I look at his face, a smile seems to play on his lips. People may think this is madness. So be it. How beautiful! How exquisite! How ecstatic! Sometimes in the privacy of my room, I dance while singing *Guru Om, Guru Om*. Sometimes I feel that my beloved's head is swaying in the photograph. Such madness of love arises within me! The pulsation of his ecstasy pervades my entire body like the movement of the wind. I have become what I wanted to become. Still, my addiction has never left me. The blessings of the Guru are wondrous and extraordinary.

How did I become so hopelessly addicted? After pondering this question for a long time, I finally realized that he himself had entered me in the form of that word. The power of the Self had entered me. The *kriyās* were his, the yoga was his, and meditation took place because of him. It was he, the embodiment of Consciousness, who emerged from the Blue Pearl. The final message that I received was from him. I have come to understand that he is the bliss of infinity, the bliss of love, the bliss of perfection, the bliss of the Supreme, and the bliss of the Self. What an extraordinary discovery!

Now I completely understand my addiction. It is his radiance in the light of my eyes. It is his utterance in the speech of my tongue. Through my breathing, it is he who comes in and goes out. It is he who eats, drinks, hears, and makes me hear. The power of his word permeates each of my blood cells. The fluids of my entire body are his. That is why I am joyful. I now understand that what I considered to be myself was totally unreal. I had made an error in calculation and was trapped in it. The truth is that Gurudev himself had entered me through that word.

Ah, what power that word had! Gurudev entered me and replaced all my bodily fluids with his. How powerful he is! He evicted me and took up residence himself. He annihilated my ego. Now I understand that this was why I became addicted to him. My Guru entered me, and who knows where he disposed of me? By making my individuality his, he became me. This is the Guru's compassion.

HE KEPT
WORKING ON ME

*A*lthough the Guru has great gifts to give us, he can give them to us only when we become worthy of receiving them. I can tell you this from my own experience. For several years I kept coming and going from my Baba's place. When I was there, I would become restless, so I would leave and go somewhere else for a while. The reason for this was ego and pride. Nityananda was a being who loved to challenge others, and I was a person who was too proud. At his place people used to line up, waiting for hours to receive something from him. He was always established in the supreme state. Sometimes he would return to the normal state of awareness in a particular mood, pick up something, call someone close to him, and give him that. Whatever *prasād* he gave people was like a wish-fulfilling tree that would fulfill all their desires. I waited to see if I would receive anything. Nothing — not even a glass of water. Sometimes he would pick up something and say, "Come here," and I would go running. Then he would say, "Not you. I'm calling someone else." In that way, he would insult me in front of everyone again and again, and I would die. The bigger my ego was, the worse the insults became. This went on for several years. He kept working on me, and I kept coming and going. I would leave, but then I would miss him and come back. He would work on me some more and I would leave. But I would remain tranquil, thinking, "If I get something, that's fine; and if I don't get anything, that's fine too." The more my Guru tested me, the more I advanced in my sadhana. No matter how much he tested me, I did not look for faults in him. Instead, I looked for my own faults. I asked myself, What do I lack? What are my shortcomings?

Finally, after a long time, he gave me something, and through his grace I attained what I had been seeking. But it was only after I had become a disciple that I was able to receive his gift.

We cannot attain the full grace of the Guru unless we become disciples. The great saint Brahmananda said, "Become ashes at the Guru's feet and then you will meet God." We have to allow the Guru to work on us, we have to dissolve our ego and pride at his feet. We may adopt a particular Guru and keep his picture on our wall and feel something when we look at it. We may have certain experiences when we meet that Guru. But if we want to be totally transformed, if we want our heart to be washed of all the filth that has accumulated there, if we want to attain everything the Guru has to give, we have to offer ourselves to the Guru without reservation. This is what it means to become a disciple. Just as you give a piece of clothing to a launderer and let him do whatever has to be done, you have to give yourself to the Guru completely and permit him to remold and reshape you in whatever way he likes.

What does giving yourself to the Guru mean? It does not mean having to stay very close to him or having to give him all your money or having to leave your family and your job and follow him wherever he goes. Nor does it mean becoming small and wretched, expecting someone to take care of you. To give yourself to the Guru means to constantly try to imbibe the Guru's instructions.

❧

In India there is this fruit called mango, and it is a wonderful thing. It is revered in our country. One day my Baba told me not to eat mangoes. So I didn't eat mangoes for twelve years, but I had to do sadhana under a mango tree. I used to sit in that tree and under that tree. Eventually I accomplished everything under the mango tree. One day, twelve years later, my Guru gave me a mango. I ate a mango on that day, and that was it — never again.

So I did sadhana in a very, very disciplined manner. When you follow the Guru's words, you attain everything. Not only this, when you follow his words, he enters into you completely. The Guru's grace is also called the lotion of Consciousness. Once this lotion is applied to your eyes, you accomplish everything.

Afterward, when I was given the ashram, I planted mango trees everywhere, and people who come to the ashram get to eat them. Even now in front of my seat in the ashram there is a mango tree. And in the gardens you will find mango trees, because under a mango tree I attained everything.

❧

I did not make any overt gestures to please my Guru. I pleased him from within by obeying his wishes and commands fully. When I would sit for meditation, different lights would appear: the red light, the white light, the black light, and finally the blue light. Then a golden saffron light would appear, and the Guru would appear within that light. I would then receive instructions from him.

The more I watched the blue dot, the more I loved it. The more I loved it, the happier I became. I thought I had attained everything. I began to revel in that blue dot. At this point I was very proud and I went to meet my Guru. He said, "You have a long way left. Go! Just go! Right now, leave this place."

So I turned away and went back. Once again, I became absorbed in meditation. I received a lot of understanding from that Blue Pearl.

⁂

*O*ne day in Gurudev's presence, I referred to someone as a crook. Immediately Gurudev said, "Hey, Muktananda! Is there really any crooked person in this world? It is just the crookedness of your cleverness. Everything is the pervasion of the supreme Truth. God has created the play of the world for His own pleasure. No one in the world is crooked." Ah, how perfect he was. What Siddhahood!

He continued, "O Muktananda! You are seeing with petty understanding. With this kind of awareness, you are heading in the wrong direction. Change your outlook. Correct your understanding. Then see that the world is just a play, an entertaining movie. It is neither true nor false. Know this secret. Only then will you attain something." What a great teaching that was, and how absolutely true. What divine wisdom of the Self. This is the teaching of the compassionate Siddha Guru.

Another time when I was near my Baba, someone made a mistake, and I remarked very softly, "Hey, you fool!"

Baba heard me and said, "Come here. When was a fool ever created? When this universe came into existence, God created everything, so everything is God. When did He create a fool? When did that happen?"

I had no answer.

"You saw your own foolishness in him."

"Thank you," I said. "It's true. I saw my own foolishness in that person."

So the world is as you see it. You project your own outlook onto someone else, onto this entire creation. Otherwise, this world is nothing but God. Everyone is an image of the beautiful Lord. Everyone is a flame of the supreme Truth. Therefore, over and over again I say, "With great respect and love I welcome you all." Why? Because everything is the Truth.

*W*hen I was doing sadhana, I came across a person who was teaching *riddhis* and *siddhis* — how to attain supernatural powers. I studied under him for a while. He had the power to materialize a train or bus ticket. Of course, it was a fake ticket. He could also tear a piece of paper and it would become a five rupee bill — for five hours. Afterward, it changed back into plain paper. He could transport a piece of apple from one place to another. If someone had something in his pocket, he could transfer that object into someone else's pocket. It was all fake, it was phony. It wasn't God's grace, it was just a mediocre skill. It meant nothing.

Having learned all these tricks, I went to see my Baba. The moment I entered my Baba's place, he took out a long stick and began to scold me. He said, "You thief, you traitor, you rogue! What are you doing here? Get out of here!" I fled.

Then I began to think about it. He called me a thief? He called me a traitor? I never stole anything. I never betrayed anyone. Why did he say that? So I returned and peeked in. I really wanted to be with him. He got the stick out again and shouted, "You unworthy fool! Get out of here." I fled again.

I began to think about it. I hadn't done anything like that. Why would he say such a thing about me? I was really upset; I felt that my heart was going to burst.

Finally, my right understanding told me it did not matter what he did. The Guru's anger, the Guru's curse, the Guru's blessing — they are all the same; they are nothing but a bestowal of grace.

So I gathered myself and with great courage I went inside again. He had already thrown the long cane in my direction, so it wasn't close enough for him to reach. But he still had one more — a little one — and he hit me very hard with that, saying, "Will you ever do that again?" He hit me so hard you can't even imagine.

With great humility, I said to him, "I don't understand what mistake I've made."

"Didn't you learn those phony supernatural powers?" he said.

"Oh, yes." Then I promised, "Never again, never again."

"In your entire life, will you ever use those supernatural powers? Will you ever try to fool others with those phony powers?"

And I said, "No."

Then he told me, "A *sādhu*, a holy being, is totally absorbed in his own Self, totally immersed in his sadhana."

❦

There was a man called Narielwala Baba, the Baba with the coconut, who fell into the trap of performing marvels. What he would do was have people bring him a coconut, then he would break it open, and the answer to their question would be in the coconut. It was never a true answer. If they wanted a child, the answer said they would have a child, but no child ever came. If they wanted money, the answer said that they would get money, but they never did.

Now Narielwala Baba and I love each other very much and he comes to the ashram twice a year. The first time he came was during the days of my Guru, Bhagawan Nityananda. My Baba had a very strange disposition. Unless he was approached properly he would lose his temper. He was so hot-tempered, in fact, that most people would not go near him. They would stand at a respectable distance because they were scared. Even I was scared of him and would not go too close.

If he lost his temper he would pick up anything lying nearby and hurl it at you. He was an *avadhūt*, a divine saint of the highest order, beyond conventional standards. He wore only a loincloth and sometimes a blanket. But those who had eyes to see could see that that blanket held the entire universe.

One day, Narielwala Baba showed up at his place. When Nityananda saw him, he started to abuse him violently and picked up a rock and went after him, shouting abuses the whole time. Narielwala ran away in terror. When he reached my place, which was a short distance away, he was perspiring and shivering with fear. He called frantically, "Muktananda Swami! O Muktananda Swami!"

I came out and asked what happened. "Gurudev flew at my throat with a stone in his hand. I don't know why I enraged him so. And he shouted, 'false miracle-monger' at me. I am still shivering, he has frightened me so."

"Don't be afraid. Don't be upset. A great being blesses you even through anger," I told him. "Whether Baba Nityananda hits you or showers his affection on you, both of his acts are going to promote your true welfare, so don't worry."

This made him relax a little and convinced him that he wasn't doomed because he had enraged such a great saint. After some time he confessed that he hadn't eaten anything and was feeling very hungry. He asked me if I had any food, and I said, "I am going to give you two big coconuts. Break them and materialize food and both of us will have a good meal to our hearts' content."

Narielwala Baba confessed, "Well, I can't produce anything to eat. I can only produce things to show people."

"That's why Nityananda Baba was enraged and went after your throat."

Anyway, I fed him.

*In India, there were many yogis who were able to manifest the power of levitation. They had to spend a lifetime learning how to do it, but it's not so extraordinary. They awaken the Kundalini energy through *pranāyāma*, and then they practice three yogic locks or *bandhas*. They stay in these positions for a very long time. The fire of yoga eventually burns up the water and the earth elements in the body. These are the two elements that make the body heavy, so when they are burned up, the person can levitate instantly. It's a strenuous practice. My Babaji was able to do it. I wanted to learn it too. But while I was practicing it, he said to me, "You don't need to learn that — birds fly higher anyway."

READ YOUR OWN
INNER BOOK

*A*t one point in my sadhana I discovered that knowledge is man's true nature. Shaivism says, "When pure knowledge arises in man, he attains the Lord." So I began to read books — many, many books. I used to stay a mile away from my Gurudev's place, and when I went to see him, I would take a book under my arm.

My Babaji watched this for a long time. He must have wondered whether I was ever going to stop reading. But there was no way I could stop reading. It wasn't that I was holding on to the book — the book was holding on to me. Whenever you have an addiction, that's what happens. Whatever you're addicted to holds on to you.

Finally, one day he called me closer and said, "Hey, Muktananda, come here. What's that you're carrying under your arm?"

"It's an Upanishad," I said.

"Dust!" he said. He was very fond of this word "dust." He would describe everything as dust. He went on, "Do you know how this book was written? Books are created by someone's mind. The mind creates books. Books have never yet created even a single mind. Where is your mind? Where has it gone? Instead of reading someone else's mind, meditate and then read your own mind. Put this book aside and meditate. Meditate a lot. When you meditate a lot, true knowledge will spring forth from you. You won't have to read books. Inner knowledge is far superior. Write your own book with your own mind. Meditate. Many books will come out of you."

The truth of what my Guru was saying dawned on me immediately. This truth will dawn upon you too when you tap that center of knowledge within yourself. So far, you are dwelling only in the eye center, which is the center of the waking state, and the throat center, which is the center of dreams. You haven't yet reached the heart center, which becomes active during meditation.

There is a center of knowledge, a creative center, within, and when you reach that place of knowledge, great poetry and literature spring up spontaneously. That is how the scriptures were

composed — the Koran, the *Gītā*, the Bible, the *Dharmapāda*. All the scriptures emanate from this center of knowledge. Some people reach a little part of this center; others reach a bit more, but it is very hard to gain the whole center of knowledge.

The inner Shakti, when it is awakened, is the great treasure of knowledge. No one has any greater knowledge than that Shakti. When it awakens within you and inspires you, you can become a great scholar.

How can you experience your own inner Truth in outer books? Books may be able to draw the map of the inner Truth. But how can you experience That without going inside? My Gurudev was a being who would make you open your own inner book and read that.

WORSHIP THAT ON THE INSIDE

I had great liking for the *Rudram*. I had become so addicted to it that I would go to a riverbank, regardless of where I was, collect sand, and make a *lingam*. While sprinkling water on it from my water bowl, I recited the hymn. I also recited the *Rudram* in the little temple next to where the Samadhi Shrine is now. I would go there very early, take a bath in the hot springs, then go inside the temple and read the *Rudram*, and finally I would go to meet my Baba.

One day, he called me close to him and asked, "Where did you come from just now?"

"I did a little bit of puja."

"Where did you do the puja?"

"In the Temple. I performed *abhishek*, and I did some worship."

"Why are you doing that? There's a *jyotirlingam*, an image of light, inside you. Have you worshiped that? Only one who doesn't understand worships the image on the outside, but one who does understand worships That on the inside. From now on, you should worship That on the inside. What is there in the outer image? Worship the deity in the heart. Give Him a holy bath."

I never did that worship again. I stopped performing mental

worship to the *shivalingam* and I began to render it to my Guru, Nityananda Baba. I would install him in all the different parts of my body — in my feet, my legs, and thighs, and so on — and thus I would achieve complete identity with him, complete oneness with him. And thinking myself to be Nityananda, I would meditate.

My Baba would never allow anyone to take his photograph, so people had to hide to take his picture. They also had to receive his abusive words. I was the first to persuade someone to take his picture, and he abused me a lot. In the morning he would walk down the hallway, so I had a photographer set up an automatic camera on the wall. While Nityananda Baba was walking, the flashbulb went off. He was really angry.

The photographer became petrified with fear and began to repent. I was standing some distance away, but I could see him turning cold. I went up to him very quietly and said, "Don't be scared, don't worry. We'll talk to him. Nothing will happen. Those abusive terms don't mean anything. Nothing will go wrong, everything will go right with us."

After my Baba finished his walk, he went inside and sat down. I went inside with the photographer and sat down in front of him. "Baba," I said, "someone made a big mistake and took a photo of you. If you don't talk to him, he will die within a short time."

"Where is he?" he asked.

"This is the man," I said.

And that is the story of the first photograph of Nityananda Baba.

There was one particular photo of my Baba that I used to look at all the time. I would focus on it in meditation. One day I had finished my meditation and stood up to do an *āratī*. When I was almost finished, the glass on the photograph broke into pieces. Immediately, I felt that he was going to leave his body very soon. Two weeks later, he left.

On Tuesday, August 8, 1961, my Baba left his body. The night before, he called me very close to him. Usually I sat far away from him. But that night he called me very close to him. He called me inside. He had never, never shown me so much love, but that night he showered me with love. He also moved his hand on my head for a long, long time. The people there were amazed and pleased because he never did that to anyone. Then he put his hand inside my mouth a long way. (I don't know how he did it.) He gave me the final *dīkshā*, the initiation of the Siddhas. And finally he said, "The entire world will see you one day."

I knew that he was going to leave his body very soon. I became as still as a tree. We sat there for a long time: I motionless, and he with his hand on my head. I can still feel the place where it rested. What he gave me will never leave me. What he put inside will always remain there, and it will be effulgent.

My Guru was such a great being. When he was alive, I wasn't aware of meditation, yoga, pain, or pleasure. I was completely absorbed in him because he was there. I led my life with great ecstasy. At that time I never thought of my future. He left his physical body, but he is still with me in his subtle body.

GURUDEV SIDDHA PEETH

*W*hen I took *sannyāsa*, I took a sacred pledge, chanting a mantra before a fire and holding water in my hand, that I would never build up an ashram, that I would roam happily in bliss and live under the trees. Such a vow is of the greatest importance, and if you break a vow that you take at the time of *sannyāsa*, then you go to hell. I haven't gone to hell, but I could have gone there. I am not joking.

Many people wanted me to run their ashrams, because they were so impressed by my radiance and liveliness, my energy and intelligence; they were certain that I would run their ashrams very well. But I did not get involved anywhere. Even after coming to Ganeshpuri, I did not stay in my Baba's ashram. I used to stay outside the temple at Vajreshwari.

Then I developed great love for Baba, and one day Baba asked me, "Do you want to have a Guru?" The question actually meant, "What does it mean to have a Guru?" At that time I thought that having a Guru meant that you received initiation from him, you received a mantra from him, and then you practiced meditation under him to have the experience of samadhi, and so on.

Baba said, "Having a Guru means something entirely different. Having a Guru means that you surrender yourself completely to the Guru and do his bidding most faithfully."

Then after a month he asked me to accept this piece of land.

"In whose name?" I asked.

"In your name," he said.

I answered, "I took a vow at the time of *sannyāsa* that I would never own a piece of land and never build up an ashram." But the Guru was saying: Take it. So I took this piece of land. It was he who paid for it. The present temple and kitchen and meditation rooms are situated on the piece of land given by him. This is how the ashram started, and you know how it has grown.

I was obeying the will of my Guru, so in spite of having broken the pledge I had taken at the time of *sannyāsa*, I did not go to hell. This is *aniccha prārabdha karma* — it was determined, not by my will, but by someone else's will. The ashram was built up by his will, not my will.

⁂

I fully believe what the *Gītā* says: Mysterious are the ways of karma. Man plans one thing out of pride, egoism, and conceit, but God wills something entirely different. A little health, wealth, learning, and power seem to make a person so bold that he begins to advise and teach even God Himself. But my firm belief is that the divine will is bound to prevail.

My fondest desire during the days of my mendicancy was that I should be constantly on the move, like flowing water. For this reason, I continued to wander throughout the country without settling down. But how could I hold my own against God's or the Guru's will? One can hardly achieve anything by imposing one's own will on things. I finally had to settle down at Gavdevi, following the urgings of destiny, the will of God, and the command of my Gurudev; and I accepted this. Then I had to run an ashram and I also accepted this. While setting up Shree Gurudev Ashram, I was confronted with many obstacles, difficulties, and hurdles, yet the ashram came into being with ease. The reason was that I never personally wished to establish an ashram; it was all divinely willed. I never thought that I would have such a big place, but that's the way destiny wanted it.

⌘

My Guru used only a few words, telling me, "Stay here." At that time no one knew what the implications were. Those few words included this magnificent ashram, with the kitchen and all the devotees from here and abroad, and so many other things. Those words that he uttered were so simple, that at that time even I didn't anticipate that all of this would happen. So there is absolutely no point in worrying about things or in anticipating anything.

Since I rely absolutely on my Guru, on God, there is no need on my part to worry about the future because whatever has to happen will happen, the persons who are going to execute those things will arrive at the right time, and everything will happen automatically.

This lineage will never be broken. Baba Nityananda, my Guru, gave me his work to do. Similarly, when I leave this world, I will have to make someone else responsible for the work.

PART THREE

You Are All the Nityananda Family

CHAPTER NINE

The Air I Breathe

I adore my Guru, Bhagawan Nityananda. It was through his grace that I realized who I am. It was through his grace that my spiritual journey was fulfilled. From a beggar, I became a king. My Guru is more alive to me now than when he was living. He comes from Siddhaloka and gives me messages. It is he who appears in different forms to my devotees and directs their sadhana. He is the air I breathe. He is my life. He is my innermost reality.

There are seekers who tell me that when they sit for meditation in front of my picture, they have a vision of Nityananda. There are others who tell me that as they look at me, I seem to dissolve into Nityananda, and that they see him permeating every fiber of my being. It is Nityananda who entered me in the form of Shakti; Muktananda is no longer here.

Even after he has left his physical form, the Guru continues to exist for his disciples. There is nothing to fear. The Guru lives in the *sahasrāra* as much as he lives outside. I get letters from many seekers in my own country, and from other countries as well, who say that in their meditation they had a vision of Nityananda Baba and received guidance from him. Then they saw Muktananda Baba — and I don't even know these people. Many of them describe how Nityananda came into their dream or revealed himself in some way, or how he cured them from illness or gave them a mantra or awakened their inner Shakti.

If you read the scriptures, you will find yogis or divine incarnations assuming different forms for all kinds of tasks that need to be performed in various places. My Baba used to guide his devotees in far-off countries such as England and America. Once he even gave guidance in a vision to a man traveling by plane. Chiti Shakti is unfathomable in Her potency and full of infinite miracles. Depending on a seeker's sincerity, faith, and confidence, the Shakti makes him fearless. According to his feelings and understanding, the Shakti even instructs and guides him in the form of the Guru.

The Guru dwells in his particular form for a very long time. All the Siddhas who dwell in Siddhaloka dwell in their own particular forms for a long time. The people who see my Baba in their meditations and dreams can bear this out.

⁕

If you want to know who my Baba was, you'll have to become like him. With the power of love, a person should try to enter inside himself to know what Nityananda was, to know his state.

For me, my Baba is not far away; he is very close to me — very, very close to me. For me, he hasn't left. He is still with me. He has permeated my entire being from head to toe and is in every pore of my body, in every blood cell.

⁕

*E*very day we recite a mantra that begins *nityānandāya gurave*. We should pay close attention to it. These two words mean that Nityananda is the Guru. Often people confuse the Guru with a teacher or a person who gives you some instruction. But the Guru is not only one who teaches; he is also one's own inner Self, and at the same time he is the supreme Lord.

The Guru's name — Nityananda — has a deep significance. The first element of his name is *nitya*. *Nitya* means eternal, everlasting, permanent. The permanent is that which remains the same in all places, in all times, in all forms, and in all substances. Everything else is impermanent.

What is present in America but not in India cannot be considered to be *nitya*, and what existed two hundred years ago but does not exist anymore cannot be considered to be *nitya*. What is present in a body but not in this flower cannot be *nitya*. He who dwells changelessly in all places; in all things, high and low; in all times, past, present, and future, is *nitya*, is permanent.

The Guru is not only everlasting, but also *ānanda*, supremely blissful. In fact, his true nature is bliss. He is the one who delivers his disciples from bondage, from affliction and suffering.

Nityananda is the inner Self who activates our *prāna*, who digests and assimilates all that we eat and drink, and thus sustains us. He is the inner inspiration of the Kundalini energy. He is our very *prāna*, our very life. He is the very source of our vitality, the very source of our essence. He is that which is fully conscious, which is perfect.

DO YOU SEE
THE MIRACLE?

A Guru looks like a human being to the physical eyes, and it is very difficult for an ordinary person to see God in that human body. Ordinary people say, "He eats like us, he drinks like us, he sleeps like us, he laughs like us and has fun like us." My Baba loved to play with little children. But in a Guru's body, there is this Shakti, this divine force that is completely alive. That is what makes a Guru. As you follow the words of the Guru, the Shakti enters you more and more and more, until one day that Shakti transforms your being into the being of the Guru.

Within every person there is this Shakti. It is the divine power, God's power. And it is only because of this power that we live. This power is also known as the Self or God. As long as you do not know the Self, no matter how much you try to improve on the outside, you cannot really improve.

People used to go to my Gurudev and ask, "O Gurudev, I want

to see God! I want to see God!" My Gurudev would say, "Just look around! Everyone is God! Everyone is God!"

Every one of you experiences this, but you do not understand it. You do not know how He resides within. When you are awake, you perform so many actions, but there is One within who witnesses all your actions. When you go to sleep and dream, there is One within who remains awake and watches all your dreams. If you know that One, if you know that Knower, then you know everything.

⁕

The Guru pervades everything — every sentient and insentient thing. Sometimes when Nityananda gave darshan, someone would say, "Oh, Baba, it's been so long since I've had your darshan!" And Baba would say, "Why? Wasn't I where you were? Wasn't I in the things you were seeing? Wasn't I in the people you were seeing? Your father is Brahman, your mother is Brahman, you are Brahman. All are Brahman. Everything is Brahman. Where else do you look for Him?"

Once I went with my Guru for a walk along the bank of a river. Near the road was a huge rock. He said, "Do you see this rock? See the miracle? See the doing of the universal Consciousness? Here it has become a rock, here it has become a human being, and here it has become a tree. But although it has become all this, it does not lack Consciousness in its fullness."

He used to say, "All are Rama — great as well as small. Rama is yours. Rama is mine." This is truly the essence of Vedanta. Nityananda had seen the mystery of things. He was fully aware of the inner Observer, the One who understands. His skill in practical affairs was based on the Vedantic vision of unity in diversity. He would say, "Neither go toward another, nor move away from him. Neither become hostile to anyone, nor run to strike up friendships. Do not rush to accept a gift, nor become entangled in the pride of giving. Do not look for faults in others, nor congratulate yourself on singing their praises. Shun evil completely, but do not at the same time become attached to good. Every moment utter, 'O Rama! O Rama!' Never forget Rama. Think of God and not of yourself."

"Regarding praise and blame as brothers, continue to repeat, 'O Rama! O Rama!' Destitution should be as welcome as riches. Both of them are the fruits of past actions. They affect one who identifies himself with them. Remain detached from both since they are the consequences of destiny determined by karma and are the will of God. Do not prefer one to the other, and thus avoid being pseudo-wise. Do not set yourself up as a worthless middleman who snatches from the rich and distributes to the poor. Do not become agitated by either the riches of the wealthy or the poverty of the poor. Constantly utter, 'O Rama! O Rama! O Rama!'

"Putting on the guise of the love of Rama, you claim to be a follower of Rama, yet you resort to the malicious distinction of high and low. Open your eye of knowledge and see what you should do. You have sought initiation in the outlook of equality, but your actions reek of partisanship, of inequality. This is a mockery of devotion and knowledge. Do not behave like this. It is Rama who appears in different guises. Continually repeat, 'O Rama! O Rama!'

"This world is Rama's playhouse. There cannot be a king without subjects. There cannot be riches without poverty. There cannot be day without night. The universe is based on duality. Duality will vanish only when the universe vanishes. O renunciant, why have you given up repeating the name of Rama and turned to other things instead? Why should you take sides in any way? Realize that it is Rama who weeps and Rama who laughs. Why do you abandon the name of Rama? Keep repeating the divine name of Rama. Rama's will alone works. Much of your life has already been spent fruitlessly. Not much time is left before you die. Why do you perceive differences in Rama? All is Rama; all is Rama indeed."

This is what Nityananda Baba used to say.

WHATEVER IS YOURS IS IN YOU

Everything is inside you. When God Himself dwells in your heart, then what can't you attain? You must have this awareness that the supreme Truth that is there in my Gurudev Nityananda is also inside you in the same measure. The one who is the Truth has become all men and all women. He has become two only to perform daily activities because he cannot do so as one. He is the Guru and he is also the disciple. There is nothing other than That; everything is pervaded by God.

People ask me, "What will happen when you leave?" But I can't leave. I live right inside you in the form of Consciousness. So have this perfect understanding. I will meet you inside yourself all the time. We have been together for a long time. You are mine and I am yours. If you have real understanding, then I am with you all the time, no matter where I go.

You can see that Truth inside yourself right now. That Truth is you as well as me. God is inside you, yoga is inside you, the mantra is inside you. What are you looking for outside? Be happy with your Self, be in your own ecstasy. Understand and see everything inside yourself. Don't look for it outside. I bless you all. I also bless you that the meditation and wisdom of the inner Self may come to you all. I love you!

The Self is pure, perfect, and always satisfied. It never touches sin, virtue, or impurity of any kind. The Self is the embodiment of all the gods and sacred places. The Self is called Consciousness and the highest Truth. Let that Self revel with bliss in your heart — this is my greatest wish.

People try to purify the Self, which is already pure. They make efforts to attain the Self, which is already attained. The truth is that this world is permeated by the Self. Whatever we see and whatever is seen in this world is only the Self. Because of our wrong understanding we see impurity in purity, imperfection in perfection, bondage in freedom, and then we become miserable even in happiness. This is because we are ignorant of the knowledge of our true Self.

O my beloved brothers and sisters, who are my own Self, you were pure when you were born. Living in the world does not affect your purity. Even at the end your purity is never contaminated. I do not look upon you as just my devotees or disciples. I consider you all sisters and brothers in the family of my Nityananda Baba.

You are all pure souls. You were born pure. Your perfection is already with you. Each of you is a flame of that pure Self. Being of the family of Nityananda like me, you have joined me to do his work. You are me and I am you. This is the vision of Siddha Yoga and this is the knowledge imparted by Nityananda. Not only am I your Self, you are also my Self. Your *prāna* is my *prāna* and your life is my life.

Do not get involved in "mine and thine," "this is small and this is big," "this is yours and this is mine." Do not create such divisions. Keep working without ego or pride. If the feeling of "mine and thine," "small and big," arises in you, and the desire to raise someone up and bring another down, then you can be sure that you are falling.

Keep meditating regularly. Keep repeating your mantra with discipline. Keep hugging the sisters and brothers of our Nityananda family, and keep pouring forth love on each other. Love is the Self, love is religion, love is God, love is the path, love is the only thing of great value to acquire.

Nityananda is universal bliss. Let him always swell in your heart in the form of bliss. Do not forget the final message of Nityananda: Meditate on your Self. Worship your Self. Kneel to your Self. Remember your Self. Whatever is yours is in you.

ALL COUNTRIES
ARE HIS

*T*he religion of the Self is the highest religion. The scriptures say, "What is higher than the Self that could be loved, that could be honored, that could be worshiped?" This is what Nityananda taught me and this is what I travel abroad to tell people. I saw the Supreme Reality in my own *sahasrāra*, and I see it in everyone. For me, there is no truth greater than that.

Before I went to the West, I waited until I received Nityananda's command. I first had to receive my passport from him. It would have been useless to go without having been sent by him. There would have been no joy in it. Besides, there would have been no point in traveling without his command — people come to Ganeshpuri from all over the world. Whenever I went abroad, it was because I was sent by Nityananda, and it was through his grace that I could do so much good work when I traveled.

Those who have little understanding think that one country is different from another, but all countries are his, all paths are his, all languages are his, and all men are his relatives. In God's house there is no particular religion or sect or faith. To Him, all are the same.

⁂

The whole world, from the primordial Guru, Shiva, down to an ordinary blade of grass, is Nityananda. No matter what ashram, faith, or country you may belong to, remember that all countries, ashrams, faiths, whatever exists or does not exist now, and whatever will take place in the future are all nothing other than the sport of Nityananda.

With firm faith in the Self, I say again that as far as I am concerned, no one is junior, no one is senior, no one is good, and no one is bad. Everything is the sport of Nityananda. Understand this sport thoroughly. On the outside one may be ignorant or learned, rich or poor, but no such differences exist in the Self. How can there be any alteration in the Self? If you perceive such a thing, know that you are deceiving yourself.

Even though I may appear to see differences in daily life, my vision is beyond all differentiation and is the embodiment of Nityananda. It is my firm faith that the entire world is nothing but Nityananda. The world belongs to Nityananda, and it is he who has become the world. He is both immanent and transcendent. This is the divine vision granted to me by Bhagawan Nityananda. This is the firm awareness of my heart. It is the supreme Truth.

HE IS FULLY ALIVE
IN ALL OF YOU

I am filled with overwhelming love and gratitude to my beloved Shree Gurudev, my Baba, for his grace. Without it nothing could have been accomplished on the travels I made. Since my Guru entered me in the form of light, the form of Chiti Shakti, he has never left me, even though his physical form is no more. He has guided me throughout every step of my life, appearing in my meditation and dreams to bring me messages. He always appears as the light of Consciousness in everyone and everything.

Although I have offered my entire being to him without reservation, it still seems very small compared to his inexhaustible grace. Sometimes when I think of him in the privacy of my room, I cannot help but dance and sing in the ecstasy of love.

When people ask me if I miss him, I say, "Yes and no." I do not miss him, because he is alive within me as a very real presence; yet I do miss him because these physical eyes can no longer behold his exquisite form. What a beautiful, radiant form he had — his humming voice, his breath that pulsated with the power of the mantra, his long tapered fingers, the laughter that shook his belly, his powerful glance, his elephant gait, his simple but bewitching smile, his deep and melodious snore, his cryptic speech — all these are indelibly engraved on my heart. I could have spent my entire life watching this manifestation of the Divine. To console myself, I keep his pictures everywhere.

He has assumed all forms. He is fully alive in all of you. When it is he who is everything and who does everything, who else is there to whom I can offer my thanks? Nevertheless, it is all of you who, serving as such pure and willing instruments, have made the work of sharing Siddha Yoga so successful.

You have all worked with such devotion that you have made the impossible a reality. Wherever I went, you created a paradise. Your love has provided me with whatever I needed to carry out my Baba's work.

Do you know that when I contemplate what you have done for me, tears of gratitude roll down my cheeks? It is amazing to watch God's infinite love taking a concrete form in all of you. I can tell you one thing: I can live without food and water, I can live without the other necessities of life, but I cannot live without your love. That love is complete nourishment for me.

My Baba, through his compassion, has drenched me in the ocean of love. As Narada said, love is nectar. You have given me love; in return, I can give only love.

O my beloved Nityananda, as I have run out of words to thank you, let me offer you this *āratī*:

> *O perfect, effulgent, eternal, indestructible Nityananda,*
> *accept this āratī!*
> *The heavens and the earth are the āratī trays;*
> *the sun and moon are its two flames.*
> *All the sandalwood trees of Mount Meru*
> *are burned for fragrance.*
> *All the flowers and plants of the earth*
> *and the waters of the seven seas adorn the tray.*
> *The unstruck sound reverberates throughout the ether.*
> *The noose of the god of death is terrified of it.*
> *You have become the four kinds of food.*
> *You are the taste as well as the one who tastes.*
> *Your temples are found in all the four directions,*
> *but your seat is in every heart.*
> *The great statements of the Vedas are the nectar of your feet.*
> *O Gurudev, I, your devotee, request the nectar of your feet*
> *so that all men and women may live free from bondage.*
> *At my Gurudev's feet,*
> *Your own, Swami Muktananda*

CHAPTER TEN

Only If You Turn Within

MEDITATE ON YOUR OWN SELF

Through meditation I received the Guru's grace, and then I found him easily. He whom I had been seeking in holy centers, caves, forests, mantras, and robes was disclosed by my Guru to be my own Self, seated in my own heart.

I saw my Guru as an ideal being, a great being. I saw him as the Self. Even now I see him in the same way. I thought he was the image of happiness, and I had great faith that he would show me how to attain that happiness, how to attain that Shakti. And that's what happened. Also, I did what he told me. He always used to say, "Go deep within yourself and meditate, and you will be happy." So I did that — I would go deep within myself and meditate, and I became happy. He used to say, "Ram is within you, Consciousness is within you, God is within you. Meditate on Him." So that's what I did.

Only you can unfold yourself; no one else can do it for you. You think it is very difficult to do; you think it is very difficult to recognize That. It is not so difficult, but only if you turn within will it become easy for you.

If a mere look at a great saint could take you across the ocean of *samsāra*, then thousands and thousands who came and had darshan of Bhagawan Nityananda, people in the neighborhood who used to meet him quite frequently and even eat from his hands, would have attained liberation.

What really matters is whether your understanding is correct or not. Therefore, before starting meditation, you should first understand the true nature of your own Self, the Guru, and God. If you could just arrive at the understanding that the Guru, God, and the Self are one and the same, then you would be in a very high state of meditation regardless of whether your eyes were open or closed, whether you were sitting in a meditative posture or moving around attending to different activities. One-pointedness on God is the same as what is called surrender to the Guru. It is also the same as what is called meditation on the inner Self.

You should meditate deeply on your own Self, not on someone else. You should have the understanding that Nityananda is in you and in me as much as he was in himself. You should not think that Nityananda was six feet tall and his body was a foot and a half wide. How can a person know Nityananda if he thinks that Nityananda is the size of that photo or that he is inside the stone of the Samadhi Shrine? A saint of Maharashtra has put it very well: "If a person sees God in only one place, who can call him a yogi?" If a person has the awareness that Nityananda is everywhere, then he is not a mere yogi but the king of all yogis.

You should understand that the disciple is not different from the Guru. Whenever you say "Guru," that means you. Whenever you say "Consciousness," that is you. Whenever you say "the Self," that is you. Everything is you.

The Guru has merged with everything, movable and immovable. Whenever I want to remember my Guru, I just look at something and I see my Guru. The Guru exists everywhere. He pervades everything.

In our meditation we should not feel that it is only the Self existing within us that is great, but we should be aware that this

Self exists within everything outside too. No matter what kind of feelings arise inside you, you should have the awareness that everything is the Guru; there is nothing but the Guru. Don't try to fight with those feelings inside.

Then just see how intoxicated you will become, how you will experience the rapture, the bliss of the Self. Then you will get meditation immediately. No matter what kind of feelings arise inside you, just say *"Guru Om, Guru Om."* Everything is nothing but the Guru.

Shaivism says that whatever is in the higher worlds is also inside you. There was a great ecstatic being called Mansur Mastana who would say, "Whatever people saw in Ram and Krishna and Allah, I saw all that in me; I saw all that within my own being." That is why the sages say you should meditate on your own inner Self.

Although I meditated on the form of my Guru, I did not only meditate on his body; I meditated on him with the awareness that he was the embodiment of the Self, and that Self also existed within me. Therefore, I always say, "Meditate on your own Self."

However, the mind has an affliction. It always wants an object to contemplate. A girl thinks of a boy and a boy thinks of a girl. Something is always in your mind: your husband or wife, your child, your pet, your car, or some other object. We have become accustomed to having it this way. For this reason, I placed the form of my Guru in my mind instead of these objects. As I continued to meditate on him, I began to meditate on my own Self.

I tell everyone, "Meditate on your own Self." For the sake of my love for him, I have his statue. But I still meditate on my own Self.

Sometimes people wonder if the flow of my meditation breaks when I have to take care of details, such as thinking about *chapātis* and *dāl*, construction, and so on. The truth is that it never breaks. Just as when you are talking to me, you still remember yourself, in the same way, whatever I received through my Guru's grace and divinity remains with me no matter what I am doing. There is no way I can forget that state, because I have become That. I have become what my Guru has given to me.

When you think of Nityananda often in your meditation and merge in him, only then will you know something of him. His wisdom was very secret. He was such a being that you could receive instructions from his inhalation and exhalation.

If you remember him, no matter where you are, you can experience That. There are many people who have experienced him. Sometimes during Shaktipat you experience him. He has given me Shakti, and this is the same Shakti I transmit to you.

There are twenty-seven degrees of Shaktipat, and the Shaktipat that I received from my Guru was very divine, very great. The result is that now I can do all this work. Usually when a saint gives Shaktipat, he can give it to only two people in a week. If he does more than that, he will become very weak, he will lose all his energy. And usually he can give Shaktipat only after the aspirant has performed many austerities.

But I didn't care for all this. Whoever came to me, I gave them Shaktipat. I said, "Whatever my Guru does will happen." So I transmitted the Shakti to people all over the world. This is the power of the Guru's grace. And this is the power of *Gurusevā*.

Meditators do not really need to write letters to the Guru. If I need to ask my Guru something, he comes in meditation and gives me the answers. You can have this experience too. In your meditation sooner or later, he will certainly give you the answers from within your own being. Meditation has that much power in it. When you go deep in meditation, you get into the *tandrā* state. It is different from the dream state or the samadhi state. In the *tandrā* state you can receive answers. You have to be very alert and subtle so that you can remember them. So if you feel that you need to write a letter to the Guru, make your heart the mailbox. Just put all your letters into that mailbox, and then you will receive all the answers.

$\mathcal{M}$editate on the Self blissfully, because the Self is immortal. The Self is Jesus, the Self is Moses, the Self is Nityananda, the Self is Rama and Krishna. You can read a great deal, you can teach a great deal, and you can write and hear a great deal, but that belongs to the outer plane. Only he is in contact with the inner plane who is absorbed in the Self.

Lose yourself. To lose yourself is to find yourself. To seek yourself is to lose yourself. Understand this once and for all: There is no Shiva without you. Without Shiva, there is no you. This is the teaching of the experienced Siddhas. This is the abode of the Self. Here you can rest. This is where the saints dwell.

Remember, the body is perishable, no matter whose body it is. Eternity is only in the Self; Truth is only in the Self; greatness is only in the Self. Only the Self is worth attaining, worth seeing, worth befriending. Only the Self is worth earning. I want to tell you once again — don't attach importance to the body. How beautiful my Guru Nityananda Baba was. What a beautiful body he had! Even now if you look at him in his loincloth you feel that he is beautiful. But he had to depart. Then Muktananda will have to depart also. The entire world will have to depart.

But before departing there is one thing you must do — and that is to attain the Self. You are the Self. The Self is yours. Live forever for your Self. You are constantly thinking about your body and identifying yourself as a person. Stop! Discard that idea. Then think, "I am the Self. I am Consciousness." The fruit of thought is very great. What you attain in the end is what you think about all the time. So think, "I am the Self, I am Consciousness, I am beautiful."

The *Gītā* says that one is one's own enemy. It's true. By thinking, "I am bad, I am ugly, I am lazy," man becomes the enemy of his own Self. Why can't you say, "I am liberated; I am lovable; I am the Truth; I am the Self"? O man, why think about worthless negativities? They are dust! Why do you do that? Doctors have performed surgery on many brains and no one has yet been able to find a single fault in anyone. Why do you think that the mind's imaginings are you? Just as clouds gather and disappear in the sky, thoughts arise and disappear in the mind. Why chase them and bother yourself meaninglessly? How can they harm you? How can they touch the Self? No one can add anything to the Self, and no one can take anything away. The Self is complete and pure and perfect. Whatever you do, wherever you go, sit calmly and contemplate the fact that you are the Self. Understand, "I am the Self. I am Consciousness. I am perfect."

BECOME THE WITNESS OF THE MIND

*O*nce in India a great industrialist was brought to my Babaji. Hundreds of thousands of people worked for him. He owned a sugar mill, a motor parts factory, a tire factory, and many other businesses. But he lost his mind, and he became utterly helpless. He had to be carried in to have the darshan of my Guru. There were two doctors, two nurses, and a secretary with him. None of them could really help him. When Babaji saw him he said, "The mind is gone — everything is gone. Now, instead of taking care of others, he has to be taken care of by them, because he doesn't enjoy the grace of his mind any longer."

It was true — everything was gone. He had been the support of so many thousands of people, but now, because he had lost his mind, he could not even support his own body. This is why the Indian scriptures speak so often about the mind and how to take care of it.

The *Rig Veda* says that the mind is great. Therefore, there should be equality in your thoughts. The mind should have only good thoughts, good feelings. Almost every scripture is based on the mind. One who comes to know the ways of the mind, one who becomes the friend of the mind is a true psychologist. The mind is very vast. You can attain something only through the support of the mind.

The world exists in the movement of the mind. The external world depends on the cosmic mind, the mind of the great Self. Man exists because of the mind. My Babaji used to say, "If you have a mind you are a human being. If you don't have a mind, either you are a great being or you are a mental case."

$\mathcal{A}$ seeker once asked a sage, "Who is God? Who is the supreme Principle? Who is Consciousness?"

The sage answered, "The witness of your mind is God."

Think about this very carefully, very deeply. The witness of your mind is God. When this is the case, in what condition should you keep your mind?

Keep your mind very pure and one-pointed; do not let it wander here and there according to its own whims. My Baba used to say, "As long as the mind is fickle, one is a human being. The moment the mind becomes stable, one becomes God." This is absolutely true.

My Baba was a being who was free from the mind. Even though he had gone beyond the mind, he had not become *jada*, he had not become inert. He was very active, very conscious of everything. He knew what was going to happen in the future, and he also knew what had happened in the past. It is only the mind that obstructs your knowing these things. He also knew each and every person who went to visit him. He was free from the mind — still he knew everything.

From this you can understand that if your mind becomes pure, there is no end to the greatness you can achieve. That is why you should purify the mind. For that you need the help of the mantra and meditation.

Day in and day out our mind is always running away to imaginary worlds. It thinks and thinks for no reason. The world of fantasies is endless. It is called the *vikalpa samsāra*, the imaginary world that has no end. First one thought arises, then immediately a second thought arises which puts the first thought to an end, and on and on.

But if you become the witness of the mind, then all the thoughts, all the fantasies are destroyed, and your mind becomes still and quiet. In this world, the bound soul endures a lot of trouble and pain. The reason for this is the mind. When the mind is no longer the mind, then you become God.

God is the witness of our mind. Therefore, we should always try to turn within and know that witness. If a person can understand even the first two states of waking and dreaming, he will be able to experience God. And by knowing and experiencing God, his life is transformed.

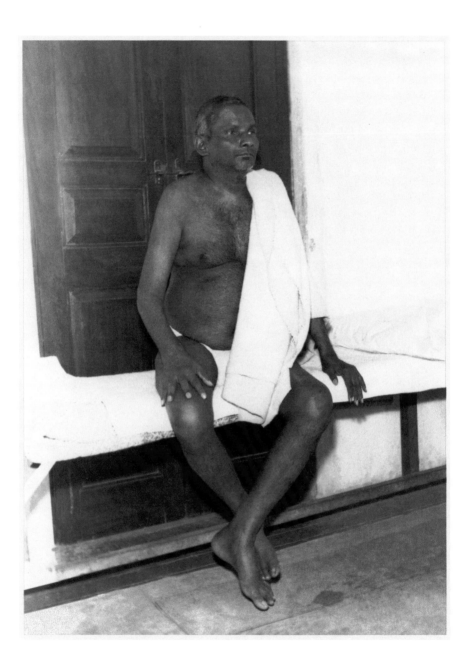

You may feel that you haven't attained God, but this is because of the weakness of your mind, the confusion of your mind. There is joy in stilling the mind; there is no joy in letting the mind run free, letting it roam here and there. When a person realizes that he is not able to do everything the mind wants him to, he feels disappointed. Then he gives up all his thoughts and desires, and he sits quietly and peacefully.

All of a sudden there is stillness in the mind. When the mind becomes still, he experiences great joy within. My Babaji used to say, "If the tendencies of the mind are still alive, how can you experience joy? If the tendencies of the mind are absent, how can you have any unhappiness?" This is Nityananda's *sūtra*, this is his great scriptural verse.

If a person cannot sit still, it is very difficult for the mind to become still. To make the mind still and steady, we should learn how to sit still. The reason you keep moving and scratching your head is the mind. To turn the mind inward, a still posture is necessary. Our Baba would rest his chin on his fist and sit that way for six hours, from early morning until noon. His mind had become steady and still in the Self. It wasn't fickle, it wasn't fidgety — it was quiet. A steady posture contains great medicine, which cannot be found in the medical system. Just by remaining still in this posture that I am sitting in now, all the seventy-two million *nādīs* of the body are purified.

Make the mind have good thoughts. A great sage said, "O my mind, always think well of others." Whether other people are good or not is not so important. But for the sake of your mind, it is important to think well of others. If the mind doesn't want to be still, it's all right. If the mind wants to think, let it think. Don't try to control it. If you try to control it, you are dumping more troubles on the troubled mind. Just change the direction of your thoughts. Make the mind have good thoughts. Then you don't have to pursue many sadhanas; then you won't be troubled much either.

I used the power of my mind to think of my Baba. Every day I used to sit before my Babaji for an hour or two. I watched his gestures, his facial expressions. I would fix my mind on him. As I did this, I was able to bring my mind under my control.

In Patanjali's *Yoga Sūtras*, there is a beautiful aphorism that describes this. It says, "If you focus your mind on a being who has risen above attachment and aversion, then you also become free from attachment and aversion." [1:37]

So if you can't control your mind, if you can't quiet it, then fix your mind on one who has risen above attachment and aversion, one whose mind has merged with the Self. Make such a being the object of your thoughts.

When my Guru was alive, what I used to do was watch him. I watched him and watched him. By watching him I totally merged into him; I transcended the duality of the mind. It is because of this duality of the mind that the world appears as a mere world.

I will explain to you the essence of thousands of scriptures in half a verse. This world is an illusion. There is no difference between the individual soul and the supreme Soul. They are one and the same. This was the teaching of Shankaracharya, who wrote:

> *This world is the creation of the mind.*
> *Once the mind becomes mindless,*
> *there is no world.*
> *There is only heaven.*

SILENCE IS THE ROOT
OF ALL SADHANAS

If you are in tune with the Guru, if you have an inner link with the Guru, you do not need any outer words from him. The Guru is not a particular body. He is the inner Self of all. One becomes a Guru only upon becoming the inner Self of all. Nityananda did not speak many words to me, but he spoke much within me and he has not ceased speaking.

My Guru seldom gave talks. But when it was necessary he would utter one single word. That single word was enough. It would act like a mantra that penetrated your entire being. A Siddha's words are just like him. The wisdom of the scriptures is sharper than the edge of a sword. You never know how the great beings will use those words. They use them to pierce the knot of ignorance, to pierce the heart.

Sometimes my Baba was asked, "Oh, Babaji, when will I attain That?" He would say, "Just as abusive terms pierce you, in the same way, my speech should enter you, it should pierce you. Then you'll attain That immediately."

Whenever I talked to my Guru, I didn't take notes. When I composed *Play of Consciousness*, whatever I had heard from him rushed up from within. It was finished in twenty days. Every word he spoke is still in my head.

Silence is the root of all sadhanas. The more you speak, the more your brain will be spoiled and the hotter your blood will become. Eventually you will lose the power of speech. Whenever my Baba spoke — even a single word — that word would not go to waste.

You never knew when he would teach something. Even if he gave just one lesson a month, it was enough for the entire year. You could learn everything from him just by watching him coming and going, sitting down and standing up. All his activities contained lessons. If you were to ask him a long question, he would answer it with a few words. If you were to nag him a little more, ask him a little more, he would turn over and go back to sleep for two hours. He contained divine lessons and everything was worth learning from him.

He was a great being, without any worries. He was very powerful. He was omniscient, but he never let anyone know that he knew everything. He was a great scholar, but he did not let anyone know that he had studied anything. You can tell from his pictures that he led a very simple life. His food was simple, and his speech was very simple also.

His teachings too were very simple; there was nothing difficult about them. He always spoke in absolutely the simplest terms, which even a child could understand. The original teaching is very simple.

He was always immersed in his own Self. On those rare occasions when he did say something, who would be present and ready with a pencil and paper to take it down? Nevertheless, there is a book in the Kannada language called *Chidākāsha Gītā*. It is a compilation from memory of certain words and sentences that Nityananda Baba had spoken from time to time while staying in south India. This book cannot be considered his, nor did he wish to say anything new.

A devotee once said to Nityananda Baba, "Give us some instruction." He replied, "What the poet-saints Narada, Mira, Kabir, Tulsidas, and others have said is just what I have said. It is not necessary for me to say any more."

My Guru didn't write any books. He used to speak a little and people have collected his words and put together some books. He spoke in aphorisms and mixed different languages together. He might say just three words, "Give this there." Give it where? There were so many places, so many people!

He used strange words. Sometimes he would say, "Hmm" — that's all. The people who had been with him for a long time could understand his words, so they interpreted them to others. For instance, they would say, "Baba said you should leave." There were times when he would speak very straightforwardly and simply.

Someone might go to him and say, "Baba, I came for your darshan." Sometimes he answered, "Hey, you dimwit! Don't I live in you? Why do you have to come here for my darshan? Have your own darshan. I am in you. Why do you have to have my darshan? Don't I live within you?"

That was his state. He was a Siddha. He was beyond rules, beyond customs, beyond disciplines. Siddhas live a strange life.

When my Baba was sitting or lying down, people would come and sit in front of him. If someone began to talk to him just for the sake of talk, he would turn his back on that person and go to sleep and begin to snore. But still when that person left him, he would be filled with joy; he would feel that he had obtained something within himself. It was not necessary for Baba to teach that person something. The Guru's silent teachings — not prattling or argument — break a disciple's doubts into pieces.

I saw my Babaji every day and spoke to him many times, but there were three times that I especially remember. The first was when I went to him and told him, "I surrender to you." He said, "Go away."

The second time he instructed me to go to a particular place to pursue my sadhana.

The third and last time was just before he left his body. He called me and spoke to me for a long time. He put his hand on my head, and then into my mouth. And through his grace I received everything.

PURSUE YOUR SADHANA

Whenever anyone approached Nityananda Baba requesting, "O Bhagawan! Please show us a new and easy path to suit this modern era," my revered Gurudev would reply, "This universe, which is a creation of Brahma, was created only once and since then nothing new has come into existence. The past era, which today we regard as ancient, was new then. Since each era undergoes changes according to the times, we perceive a particular age to be either ancient or new, but in fact, everything is now as it was in the beginning of creation."

In a kaleidoscope, loose pieces of colored glass are reflected by mirrors on all four sides. As the instrument is rotated, the glass pieces keep changing position, resulting in the appearance of new patterns, but each pattern contains the same pieces of glass. Nothing old has disappeared, nor has anything new been added.

Again, the sun is only one, but in different countries it appears to move at different speeds. In some countries the sun rises early while in others it rises late. In some places it stays longer than in others. But the sun does not have the characteristics of being late or early, of short duration or long. The sun always is as it is. The knowledge of God should be understood in the same way. It is always one; it always remains the same and it does not become more or less.

There is no question of easy or difficult paths for the attainment of knowledge. Man finds it difficult or easy according to his own mental inclinations, just as some people find the English language easy to learn and Sanskrit difficult, while the opposite is true for others.

One kind of sadhana may be suitable for one person and another kind for another person. None of these different types of sadhana is easy or difficult in itself. The yogi finds Vedanta difficult while the *jñāni* finds yoga difficult, and for the *bhakta*, both are difficult. The truth is that whatever appeals to a person will be easy for him.

*M*y Babaji used to love fun; he was an ecstatic being. He used to test people in various ways. He would give a coconut to someone and watch to see what the person would do with it. Occasionally Baba gave *prasād* right away, but most of the time he would look at someone and wonder what he would do with the *prasād*.

One day a man came and Baba gave him a coconut. The man took the coconut and sold it to a shopkeeper for fifty paisa. The man accepted the *prasād* and then he sold it! He should have eaten it immediately.

Some people had to wait for years to receive a coconut. I had to wait sixteen years. When Nityananda Baba finally gave me a coconut, of course I ate it immediately.

Whatever you learn in the ashram, digest it and put it into practice. Don't take it and give it to someone else. That's useless. Try to imbibe whatever you have learned here. Whatever you do, have the awareness of the transcendental and immanent aspects of God. Always try to see what thoughts you have inside your mind, and consider what you should be thinking. Try to explain things to yourself. A person who explains everything to himself understands everything.

*P*raise and blame have to be endured. If you receive praise or blame from the Guru, you must endure that as well. You must take it as a gift, as *prasād*. If you can do that, it will be very beneficial for you. My Guru had a very strong personality. Sometimes, as soon as he saw someone, he would utter words of abuse. But that person would be extremely pleased to have such a blessing. Sometimes people would irritate him deliberately, just to receive his blessing in the form of abuse. Occasionally he would even bless people with a blow from his stick. Then they would go away with a feeling of joy. Especially those who were suffering or in difficult circumstances in their life, they would come and surround my Babaji, hoping to get hit with his stick or by a stone.

⁂

$\mathcal{I}$ do not agree with those who identify the Guru with his physical body, or who mistake physical proximity to the Guru for inner realization. When Lord Rama and Lord Krishna were here in this world, millions of people saw them, but I don't think all of them were liberated. Sadhana is a discipline. The purer you are, the greater your sadhana is.

There were many devotees who were always around my Guru. In fact, there were so many around him that others found it difficult even to have his darshan. They were around him until his last moment, but I did not find that they gained any worthwhile state. They gained only one thing: they were always around him.

There was one boy who used to sleep very close to Nityananda Baba. His name was Rodkhya and my Baba loved him very much. Other people thought very well of him too and gave him a lot of respect. He was in charge of distributing all the gifts that people brought — food and beautiful cloth. Rodkhya ate very well and became strong and healthy. Then he grew up and became a teenager and began to go fishing every day. When Nityananda Baba called for him, people would say, "Oh, Baba, he's gone fishing." Or if it was the rainy season, they would say, "Baba, he went to catch crabs" because the crabs would be coming out.

Rodkhya would sleep near Nityananda Baba. He slept on the ground right beside his cot. But if a person doesn't know the greatness of sadhana and if he's not pure, then no matter what he does, he's worthless. That boy grew up and now sells garlands, and if he gets anything from that, that's how he leads his life.

So what's the point of mere physical closeness to the Guru if you're not sensitive to him? If you only catch crabs, how can you change? If you do sadhana, you are transformed. If you do not do sadhana, what does it matter how long you were close to the Guru? Sadhana has its own end, its own fruit. There are very few people who really do sadhana sincerely.

One must be worthy to gain the knowledge of Brahman. This worthiness is acquired by service to the Guru. But in serving, one must also have an intense desire for liberation. Without this desire, even service to the Guru will not bear fruit. Many people did personal service to my Guru for many years, but who knows what they gained spiritually?

❦

$\mathcal{M}$y Gurudev taught me to discard the notions of "my caste, my society, my people, my country." He used to say, "Why do you have to take a bath in a river or in a lake? Why don't you go to the ocean? Go take a dip in the ocean."

Jnaneshwar Maharaj said, "He is a true human being who understands that this entire world is his home. His family is the family of God. Such a person has true wisdom."

My Baba never liked to criticize any religion, sect, or person. If anyone found fault with someone else, he would say, "Hey! You have faulty vision. Ram is in all." This is the sign of a supreme Siddha.

Once a devotee of my Baba came to him and complained about another devotee. "That man drinks liquor and eats fish," he told Baba.

"So what?" Baba said. "No matter what he eats or drinks, he shits it out the next day. He doesn't hang on to it, so why should you?" No matter what you may have done in the past, you should let go of it. If the thought "I am a sinner" arises, then have another thought: "I am not a sinner. I am meritorious."

My Guru used to say that wherever a crow may go, he will not cease to be a crow. So one who is accustomed to seeing others' faults will always be seeing faults. He would see impurities even in purity. A faultfinder can never become a good seeker. To see faults in others is not a sign of a seeker.

130

My Baba would speak quite frequently about devotees who had the mentality of a crow. A crow, even in heaven, said Baba, insists on eating shit, because that is what he has been accustomed to. And this is exactly how these faultfinding devotees behave.

My Babaji always walked with his hands open, and his head used to sway all the time. The *prāna* had become still at the top of his head because of *kumbhaka*, breath retention. That is why his head would sway constantly.

There were many swamis around who would imitate this swaying of the head. They would also imitate the way he walked — he had the pace of an elephant. I watched all of those swamis, and I realized what they were doing was fake.

So sometimes when I visited my Baba, I would carry two sticks with me. If anyone's head was swaying too much, I would sit behind that person and put the sticks on either side of his head. When he asked me what I was doing, I would say, "Your head is swaying too much."

You should not imitate the Guru's outer behavior. You should attain his inner state. Then you are a perfect disciple.

My Baba's main work was to make man transcend his jivahood, his sense of limited individuality, and become established in the awareness of his Shivahood, his identity with the Lord. Thousands of people used to come to him, but I hardly saw one among them who prayed to attain Shivahood. On the other hand, I saw innumerable people asking for such mundane things as sons, money, business or employment, or to be cured from disease.

If a seeker is only interested in having the Guru remove whatever obstacles or difficulties come in his path, then he is behaving like a businessman. There was a time when businessmen in Bombay used to employ tough characters to keep the ruffians away. Those people who go to the Guru only to have the obstacles removed are using the Guru like a businessman.

I never approached my Guru for anything. I never described to him how I was at any given time, whether I was in a good or bad condition. The Guru is there to promote your highest welfare, to bring the highest good within your reach. So why expect him to help you overcome petty problems and insignificant disorders?

❦

Some of the trustees of my Baba's ashram used to talk proudly about how they had developed the ashram. The truth was that the money came as a result of my Gurudev's destiny. The architect designed and planned the ashram. The workers constructed it. But the trustees kept declaring that they themselves had created it. When visitors heard these claims, they began to wonder if the trustees had perhaps created Gurudev as well.

This is the most potent delusion in which man is entangled. A person thinks, "I have done this, I will do that," when in fact it is God who does everything.

When Lord Krishna was driving Arjuna's chariot, he held all the power. Even if Arjuna shot an arrow in the wrong direction, it would hit its target. Arjuna thought it was his doing. He didn't realize that all the time it was Krishna's power that was doing everything. After the great war had ended and Krishna had left the chariot, Arjuna was totally helpless without him.

We think we are the agents of action, but the fact is that it is some other power that makes everything happen. Out of pride each of us thinks, "It is I who am doing everything," whereas it is the Lord who is the real doer. So give up your attachment to desire, greed, delusion, anger, and pride. These passions have treated you in the most miserable manner. They have put you in their pocket. Try to escape their tyranny; try to know your true inner Self.

❦

Many devotees used to come to my Guru and many of them were his disciples. Whatever those disciples got from Nityananda depended on the intensity of their faith, the intensity

132

of their devotion, the intensity of their identification with him. The more intensely devotees identify themselves with him, the more of him they absorb into themselves.

A great devotee of Nityananda Baba used to come to Ganeshpuri from Vasai once every week for as long as my Baba was in his physical form. Now she comes here, and she brings all her children. One time she came to me, and I gave her a twig of a *tulsī* plant. She asked, "If I plant it, will it survive?"

"It all depends on the intensity of your feeling," I told her.

She went back home and planted that twig, and the next time she came she brought me flowers born from that plant.

When people came to my Guru, many would ask for grace; some would demand it. My Baba always said it is not the Guru's grace toward the disciple that matters; it is the disciple's grace toward the Guru that is of much greater importance. The moment a disciple surrenders himself completely to the Guru, the Guru's grace will be bestowed on him automatically and in full measure.

If I had really put forth disciple's grace, it wouldn't have taken me nine years of sadhana after receiving Shaktipat, nor all those other years of wandering before that. It shouldn't have taken me so long. I did not bestow disciple's grace soon enough — I was only waiting for the Guru's grace.

It was the custom around my Baba that if you were standing near him, you would not sit down until he told you to. When I went to see him, I wouldn't leave until he told me to leave. I used to watch his other devotees, and sometimes they would be standing for a long time. Sometimes Baba wouldn't tell them to leave for a day or a night, and they would miss their bus to Bombay.

Once there was a disciple called Jalandharnath, who set out looking for a Guru named Goraknath. Finally he met someone walking on the road.

Goraknath said, "Where are you going?"

"I'm looking for Goraknath," said Jalandharnath.

"Why?"

"To receive grace."

"I am Goraknath," he said. "Sit down here and I will be back." Then he left for twelve years. Jalandharnath sat there for twelve years. When Goraknath returned, his disciple had attained everything. This is the sign of a person who is worthy of receiving grace.

You can attain God, you can finish your journey, within a few years. It doesn't have to take a long time. Swami Samartha Ramdas finished his journey in twelve years. Jnaneshwar Maharaj finished his journey very quickly, in only six months. Others have finished their journeys in fifteen years, or twelve, or less. Then they became utterly content within themselves.

My Babaji used to say, "You can finish the journey like this — within a fraction of a second." And he would snap his fingers!

EVERYONE HAS HIS OWN OBJECT OF WORSHIP

*M*any people used to go to my Baba and say, "Baba, I worship you for peace." He would reply, "Do you think that you will attain peace by worshiping me? Worship your own Self, then you will attain peace."

When you worship the Guru you are worshiping him for your own sake. You are not doing the Guru a favor. For instance, if a person burns incense in front of a photograph of Baba Nityananda, it is not going to do any good to Baba Nityananda. The one who offers the incense will benefit from it. So you should worship the Guru within for your own sake. If this is your attitude, you will receive all his knowledge.

Some people worship elephants, others worship horses. There are people who worship their factories, people who worship their clothes, people who worship their shoes, and people who worship their senses and sensuality. The only difference between them and me is that I worship my Guru. Everyone has his own object of worship.

When I worshiped my Guru, I didn't give him anything. On the contrary, I received everything from him. He gave me his own Self in return for nothing.

My Guru used to drink coffee, and he invited me a couple of times to have coffee with him. Even now if you go to the

Samadhi Shrine early in the morning, you will find a few cups of coffee sitting there. People still offer coffee there, believing that it will go to my Baba. If someone were to ask them why they were doing it, they would say that this is how they like to worship their deity.

These different modes of worship are nothing but different ways to satisfy your own mind, to soothe it. As far as the Lord is concerned, He is completely full in Himself, He is beyond all worship. You can worship Him truly only when you yourself become divine, when you become one with Him. When you become completely absorbed in the act of worship, that is the highest worship.

It is the supreme teaching of Bhagawan Nityananda that the Supreme Being dwells within everyone in equal fullness, and if we worship Him in a visible form, we must not forget that we are worshiping the inner Self in a visible form. We should not think that the Self dwells outside. External worship is not true worship. It is only the worship of the inner Self which is true worship.

My Baba made me give up all forms of external worship and directed me to inner worship. If I am indulging in external worship, it is because of a certain old addiction of mine. It is because I am addicted to my love for the Guru; it is not something that he taught me. If he were still in his physical form, he would have been angry with me for worshiping him like that because he was a believer only in the inner Self.

⟨❧⟩

The inner Shakti flows particularly through the feet. In our culture when a saint arrives in someone's house, the host offers to wash the saint's feet. However, the true feet are something else. Jnaneshwar Maharaj, offering his salutations to the Guru's feet, said that the true feet are at the crown of the head in the subtle body, and he gave them the name of the mantra *So'ham*.

If anyone tried to touch the feet of my Babaji, he would get angry. I touched his feet once or twice but he really yelled at me. Still, he was full of love. A saint's blessing and anger are one and the same. Whether a saint scolds you or speaks sweetly to you, it is the same. The outer feet are all right, but it is much better if you can touch his heart rather than his feet.

My Guru never wore any sandals. However, if anyone took sandals to him, he touched them and blessed them. Then that person would worship those sandals with the feeling that they belonged to his Guru, and this feeling would bear fruit. The great sages say that God exists in the depth of your feelings. He doesn't exist merely in an idol, in wood, in clay, or in images. For this reason, there are many people who worship sandals as the Guru's sandals. No matter with what feeling you worship, it is God who makes your feeling bear fruit. In Maharashtra there was a great woman saint called Bahinabai, who said that it is the depth of your feeling that bears fruit. It is your own feeling that brings about liberation. It is the Self of all that gives the fruit of all feelings.

⁂

*T*he supreme Guru is one who can transmit his Shakti into us; who can pierce all our *chakras* and knots and fill our mind with peace and bliss. For this reason I worship my Guru with such reverence. He is as alive for me today in his statue as he was when he was in his physical form. The distinction between *saguna* and *nirguna*, the personal and the impersonal, between the animate and the inanimate, would interest only a fool. A sensible person would never be drawn toward it. It is only *gurubhāva*, or identification with the Guru, that is of the highest importance.

I still see my Guru in his same physical form, and sometimes I also hear him within. I am not an idol worshiper, and I am not fond of going to temples, either. But because I see him again and again in the same form, I have installed his statue. Once I asked him which picture of his I should worship and he suggested the one I had been thinking about. So I had it enlarged, then painted in oils, and later on made into a statue. When we worship the statue, we are worshiping him.

*M*ost of the time my Baba's eyes were closed. His eyes were very big and extremely powerful. He never looked at anyone with his open eyes. Even while eating or drinking, he used to keep his eyes closed. The photographs that you see of him were taken by a photographer who had to wait for hours and hours. When Nityananda Baba opened his eyes, at that moment the photographer snapped the picture.

A photograph has great power. What kind of power depends upon whose picture it is. The state of that person remains inherent in the photograph. I fully believe in the power of my Baba's photographs.

If you want to establish a connection with Nityananda Baba, just look at his eyes in the photograph and repeat your mantra. In this way the Shakti will enter you. Then automatically the relationship will be established.

One day a man visiting the ashram had an experience with my Guru's picture. He was looking at the photograph. Suddenly it smiled at him; then it laughed at him. The man was astounded and he wondered, "Is Nityananda trying to pull me closer to him?"

Then he turned his face away from the photo because, as he said, he was a rational person, and this kind of experience couldn't possibly be real.

When he asked me about it, I said, "How can you regard yourself as a rational person? You've lost your intelligence! If an ordinary person speaks to you, it's fine, but when the photo of a great Siddha looks at you and smiles and laughs and speaks to you, you turn your back on him! All I can say is that you're a very unfortunate being."

I firmly believe in the Ultimate Reality without any attributes or form. I adore the Impersonal, but I know fully what is good for a seeker. It is quite easy for one to accept what he can hear with his ears, what he can see with his eyes, and what he can think with his mind. But it is very difficult to accept what you cannot hear or see or think about. The only way of reaching the Impersonal is through the yoga of the personal.

Consciousness does not die. Names and forms change. It is an illusion to consider the statue of Nityananda to be mere form. However, he is attainable by devotees and disciples through the form. His body merges into the respective elements of which it is composed, but the substance is not annihilated. Those who think that the substance is annihilated do not understand the truth.

A yogi is not a worshiper of form. His objective is *nirvikalpa samadhi*. What does worship of the form lead to? What happens when the mind becomes completely still while gazing at a statue?

We worship the Guru in a personal form so that we may receive Shakti and meditate effectively, so that we may reach the journey's end. The image of the Guru is not form; it is pure Consciousness. It is beyond the distinction of *saguna* and *nirguna* because it is pure Consciousness. The mind and the senses have their pressing demands; they must have their corresponding objects. The eyes must see. That is why it is good to worship the statue or the personal form of the Guru. When the mind rises to a high state it converts the form into the formless.

❈

*B*efore India attained freedom, there were many independent princely states. When I was young, I roamed from one place to another and met a number of these rulers, and I still know some of them. But everything changes; the wheels of destiny are constantly turning. Almost all those kings passed away and even their statues have been demolished. However, the statue of my Guru, of my Baba, will last forever. It will last as long as the sun and the moon rise in the sky. No one can touch it. It will remain as it is. I saw many presidents, I saw many ministers, but I have seen only one Nityananda. The famous men all change; their names change and they don't last. But people still bathe Nityananda and worship him; they drink the water of his feet. So remember this mantra: the Guru protects you from time, from fear, and from death. I am extremely happy now because he told me to sit in Ganeshpuri and I sat there. I will sit there as long as this body lasts.

There is nothing I want now. Still, I want him, my Guru. I always keep him close to me. I keep looking at him, and there is nothing that delights me more. If you give your heart completely to the Guru, you absorb him into your heart completely.

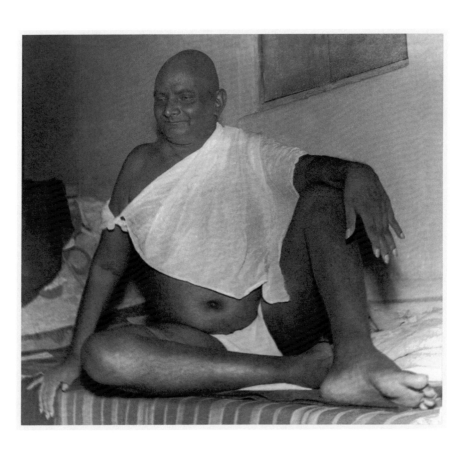

CHAPTER ELEVEN

Ambrosial in Its Very Essence

To hear about Nityananda, you will have to be saturated with supreme bliss. Only then can I talk about Nityananda. Only then will you have the capacity to hear about him. He was an ecstatic being. He had assimilated the entire universe into himself. He spoke very little. But if he spoke, he might speak for hours on end. Shaivism says that a Siddha lives in total freedom; the Siddhas are supremely free.

Many, many people sat in front of him, but they would be very quiet. He spoke to everyone but no one could hear that speech because he spoke to them from inside. People would feel, "I received something from him; I got something from him."

Sometimes my Baba would look at a person and all of a sudden he would start chuckling, and then he would laugh and his belly would shake. As the person kept watching him, he too would experience supreme bliss inside himself.

I have a lot of love for my Guru. Even though I have so much love for him, still I am afraid of him. When I look at my Guru's picture, I am afraid of him. It is fear that keeps you pure and keeps you away from bad actions, that makes you perfect in your sadhana. It is only because I had a lot of fear of my Guru — more than my devotion — that I could achieve so much in my life. The Upanishads say the fire burns only because it is afraid of God. The wind blows for the same reason. The fear that you have of your Guru or of God — that is great devotion. Even now I have fear of my Guru, even now. The more of that kind of fear I have, the more I am fearless. The fear I have of my Guru makes me fearless and brings me happiness.

I love my Baba not for his sake but for my sake. Just as an angry person suffers with that anger, even though he is angry with someone else, in the same way, a person who loves enjoys that love in his own being, even though he loves someone else.

What can I really say about my Guru? He was a being who had attained everything. Most of the time he was absorbed in his own Self. He had attained such a great meditative state that when he ate he was in that state, when he drank he was in that state, when he walked he was in that state. Just as when the river Ganges merges into the ocean and becomes the ocean, in the same way he had merged into the Supreme Principle and become That.

He was always absorbed in love. He was completely rapt in the intoxication of love. If a worthy person went to see him, he would offer him love. He was a great renunciant and very generous. He loved giving things away to poor people; he would give them clothes and food. He lived in a remote area where there were mountains all around and a few villagers. He turned the wilderness into a beautiful town.

He was omniscient: he knew the past, the present, and the future. Nonetheless, he remained very simple. He did not like people coming too close to him. He did not allow them to touch his body. Thousands of people would be sitting in front of him, but they had to be very quiet. No one could make any noise. Just by watching him, people would attain something. They would experience that Shakti.

He was such a great being. His state was so strange. Sometimes he would speak, but if he didn't want to, he wouldn't. He would use one or two words, and those words were enough for people. He would say, "Follow the right path," and that was it — a person would start following the right path. He was such a great being; the stories about him are marvelous.

He performed so many miracles but he did it very quietly. His miracles were meant for his work, for his mission. On the stage people mesmerize other people; they show off their powers. But my Guru did not display his powers. He had attained self-control. He had also attained the *siddhi* of knowing what is going on in another person's mind or heart. Even though he knew it, he wouldn't let you know that he knew it. He had equal vision for everyone. He did not take any interest in religions; all religions were the same for him.

*T*rue human religion is to welcome another person. This is true humanity — to welcome another person with love, to embrace another person. This welcome contains great mystery. God exists within everyone in the form of Consciousness. My Gurudev used to say, "God is one, and He is of the form of love." Therefore, you should learn how to welcome others with all your heart. This is the highest religion. If there is a religion that does not contain love and respect for others, then it cannot be the religion of a human being.

My Gurudev used to say all the time, "God's form is love." The Upanishads say, "God is Existence, Consciousness, and Bliss absolute." He is the bliss that exists within all of us. For this reason you should welcome another person with respect. This practice is worship; it is meditation; it is yoga, *tapasya*, and religion. If there is religion without love, then it is dry and empty and without discipline. When we experience joy in our hearts, regardless of the reason, that joy is a portion of God. It is a shadow of God's love that we experience.

Now God loves groups too. But He does not make any distinctions. He does not see east and west and south and north. We have divided everything into small pieces. We have drawn lines and created differences. But God is not like that. He is whole and complete. Everything is complete for Him. God pervades all four directions, and of course He lives in temples and mosques and churches. He also transcends all of these. Although He is everywhere, my Gurudev used to say, "He specifically dwells in a human heart." Man's heart is the divine temple of God.

Love is *bhakti*, and *bhakti* means love. The awakening of deep and boundless affection for one's beloved Guru is love of the Self, or *bhakti*. Such devotion is of the highest order and does not depend on formalities such as yogic practices, worship, rituals, or study. When the mind is desireless; when worldly objects do not attract it; when the wish for heavenly happiness and even the desire for salvation vanish and with full affection the mind is firmly established in the lotus feet of Shree Gurudev — that state of the highest, all-exclusive love is known as *bhakti*. Such *bhakti*, such supreme love, is ambrosial in its very essence. To love only Shree Gurudev with all the intensity of the heart is real *amrit*, real nectar. This *amrit* is the sweetest of all. One who receives and drinks it becomes immortal. Worldly desire is death.

An unwavering *bhakta* always longs for the ever-fresh and pure love of his Guru. No other desire remains in his heart. He longs only for Shree Gurudev. Such a *bhakta* will see the divine form of his Gurudev, hear the sweet name of his beloved Guru, and utter softly the name "Shree Gurudev." His worldly life of give and take is filled with his Guru. In short, his only longing is for the lotus feet of the Sadguru.

When such a rare longing arises by Shree Gurudev's grace, the devotee, taking full advantage of this state of blissfulness that even the sages crave, becomes free from the cycle of birth and death. His heart then becomes Gurudev's temple. The union between an ardent devotee and the beloved Guru is in itself immortality. This culmination is the height of *gurubhakti*.

All the doubts of a devotee who has attained the nectar of knowledge from Shree Guru melt away. Knowing that the world around him is the sport of his beloved Guru, he becomes free of illusions. He can go where he likes. His Gurudev appears to fill the entire world. Is there a place where Shree Gurudev does not exist? Which object is not pervaded by Shree Guru? Gurudev is the source of all animate beings as well as inanimate objects of this world. The devotee knows that the entire universe is one with Shree Guru. The basic support of the universe is the superconscious soul of Shree Guru alone. That which the Vedas describe after endless search as "not this, not this," which is even beyond the primordial sound *Omkāra*, which is the root of all forms, and in which this complete universe exists — that eternal, unknown, indestructible Principle is beloved Shree Gurudev. He is the root of all religions — self-existent, immutable, and the ruler of the universe.

Having come to know the all-pervasiveness of the Master, the devotee may stay anywhere and still devote himself to his Gurudev. He can sing the prayers of love and devotion that are inspired by his heart. Such a devotee considers time, place, past, present, here, and there to be inseparable from Shree Guru. Just as the air molds itself into any form and moves everywhere, this devotee, being enlightened with the knowledge of the Self, joyfully moves in all the three worlds.

To see and realize Shree Gurudev in all living beings is real devotion. This love for all comes through Shree Guru's grace and makes the devotee almost mad with love. He goes on singing the praises of the Master day and night. He hears, speaks, sings, and thinks of Shree Guru alone. Often, he acts in a manner that seems senseless to those who do not understand his state of divine intoxication. He remains absorbed in a state of intoxication with the Guru's love. His heart melts with extreme love and adoration for the Guru, and when this state reaches its peak, the ecstatic devotee may sometimes laugh heartily, cry, shout, sing loudly, or even dance. In this sublime state, he experiences oneness with Shree Guru.

Gurudev is sound in the ether. He alone is felt in the touch of the air. He is the light in fire, the sweetness of water, and the fragrance of the earth. He alone fills everything. He is seen in all beings in various forms. Everywhere the blessed devotee feels the same joy and nothing but joy. The entire universe is full of Gurudev Shree Nityananda, who is love — delightful and full of nectar. Everything is filled with joy, beauty, and sweetness. Devotee and God are sweet; the object and the subject are both lovable. You and I and all are blissful. All that is pervaded by delightful and lovable Lord Shree Guru is sweet. The lover of the Guru, having attained this state, remains absorbed in the nectar of divine love for all time; yet that state of love is indescribable. Love is the very essence of the innermost core of *bhakti*. Love is also an immensely valuable and cherished possession, and it is indeed the highest limit of joy and happiness. There is nothing beyond this, and that nothingness itself is Nityananda — eternal joy and bliss. Even his statue radiates powerful vibrations of his all-encompassing love. Innumerable men and women, pious and sinful, young and old, happy and miserable, still come to have darshan of his lifelike and powerful image. They consider themselves blessed, are satisfied, and leave feeling happy.

Let those with the tendency to differentiate measure what is high and what is low as if they were in a grocery store. I do not want that. My only desire is to experience Nityananda's love in everyone, to experience equality everywhere, to become a true lover in order to taste again and again the love of my Gurudev, who is established in the awareness of the Self of all. May I bow my head before such Siddhas. May I offer my ego at the Siddhas' feet.

If you really want Baba, then love everyone.
Don't see Baba only in his image,
but see him in everyone in every direction.
Then truly you will attain happiness,
you will attain peace, you will attain Baba,
and you will become Baba.
You are Baba.

GUIDE TO
SANSKRIT PRONUNCIATION

Vowels

Sanskrit vowels are categorized as either long or short. In English transliteration, the long vowels are marked with a bar above the letter and are pronounced twice as long as the short vowels. The vowels 'e' and 'o' are always pronounced as long vowels.

Short:
a as in c*u*p
i as in g*i*ve
u as in f*u*ll
e as in s*a*ve
o as in ph*o*ne
r as in w*ri*tten

Long:
ā as in c*a*lm
ī as in s*ee*n
ū as in sch*oo*l
ai as in *ai*sle
au as in c*ow*

Consonants

The main variations from the way consonants are pronounced in English are the aspirated consonants. These are pronounced with a definite *h* sound. In particular, *th* is not pronounced like the English *th*, as in *th*rone, nor is *ph* pronounced as in *ph*one. They are pronounced as follows:

Aspirated Consonants:
kh as in in*kh*orn
th as in boa*th*ouse
th as in an*th*ill
dh as in roa*dh*ouse
dh as in a*dh*ere
ph as in loo*ph*ole
bh as in clu*bh*ouse
h is an aspiration that
    repeats the preceding
    vowel

Other Consonants:
c as in su*ch*
ṅ as in si*ng*
ñ as in ca*ny*on
ṇ as in *n*o*n*e
n as in *sn*ake
ś as in bu*sh*
ṣ as in *sh*ine
s as in *s*upreme
kṣ as in au*ct*ion
ṃ is a nasal *m*

For a detailed pronunciation guide, see *The Nectar of Chanting*, published by SYDA Foundation.

GLOSSARY

Abhishek [*abhiṣeka*]
A ritual bathing offered as worship (puja) to a statue or other representation of a deity.

Absolute
The highest Reality; supreme Consciousness; the pure, untainted, changeless Truth.

Adiguru [*ādiguru*]
(*lit.*, first Guru) The primordial Guru.

Agama(s) [*āgama*]
Sacred Shaivite texts, revealed between the fourth and sixth centuries A.D., which explain religious philosophy and practices.

Ajna Chakra [*ājñā cakra*]
The spiritual center located between the eyebrows. The awakened Kundalini passes through this *chakra* only by the command (*ājñā*) of the Guru, and for this reason it is also known as the Guru *chakra*. *See also* Chakra(s).

Akbar
(1542-1605 A.D.) A great Moghul emperor who consolidated one of the most extensive Indian empires. His administrative skills, benevolent nature, and interest in culture and religion endeared him to his people.

Amrit [*amṛt*]
(*lit.*, not dead) 1) The nectar of immortality. The divine nectar that flows down from the *sahasrāra* when the Kundalini is awakened. 2) An area in Siddha Yoga Meditation ashrams and centers where refreshments are served.

Aparokshanubhuti
[*aparokṣānubhūti*]
(*lit.*, the perception of what is not invisible) A work on Advaita Vedanta by Shankaracharya, explaining God-realization as the immediate and direct perception of one's own Self by means of inquiry.

Arati [*āratī*]
A ritual act of worship during which a flame, symbolic of the individual soul, is waved before the form of a deity, sacred being, or image that embodies the divine light of Consciousness. *Āratī* is usually preceded by the sound of bells, conches, and drums, and accompanied by the singing of a prayer to the Lord with love and gratitude for all His blessings.

Ashadha [*āṣādha*]
The month in the Indian calendar when

the rainy season begins. Ashadha corresponds to June-July.

Ashram [*āśrama*]
("a place that removes the fatigue of worldliness") The abode of a Guru or saint; a monastic place of retreat where seekers engage in spiritual practices and study the sacred teachings of yoga.

Ashtanga Yoga [*aṣṭāṅga yoga*] or **Raja Yoga** [*rājayoga*]
(*lit.*, eight limbs of yoga) Eight stages of yoga described by Patanjali in his *Yoga Sūtras*, the authoritative text on *rāja yoga*. The eight stages are self-restraint, daily practices, steady posture, breath control, sense withdrawal, concentration, meditation, and union with the Absolute. *See also* Patanjali; Yoga Sutras.

Audumbara Tree [*audumbara*]
A fig tree.

Avadhut [*avadhūta*]
An enlightened being who lives in a state beyond body-consciousness and whose behavior is not bound by ordinary social conventions.

Ayurveda [*āyurveda*]
(*lit.*, knowledge of life) The ancient Indian science of medicine which teaches that good health depends on maintaining the even balance of the three bodily constitutions: wind, bile, and phlegm.

Baba, Babaji [*bābā*]
(*lit.*, father) A term of affection and respect for a saint, holy man, or father.

Bahinabai [*bahiṇābāī*]
(1628-1700 A.D.) A poet-saint of India who received initiation in a dream from Tukaram Maharaj.

Balaram [*balarāma*]
The elder brother of Lord Krishna and a participant in the battle described in the epic *Mahābhārata*, known for his strength and enthusiasm. *See also* Krishna; Mahabharata.

Bandha(s) [*bandha*]
(*lit.*, lock) A hatha yoga posture that temporarily "locks" a specific area of the body to retain the *prāna*, or life force. The practice of *bandhas* gives great strength to the body. In *jālandhara bandha*, the chin rests between the collar bones, above the breastbone; in *uddīyāna bandha*, the stomach muscles are drawn inward; in *vajra bandha*, the anal sphincter muscles are contracted and drawn upward.

Bhagavad Gita [*bhagavadgītā*]
(*lit.*, song of God) One of the world's spiritual treasures; an essential scripture of Hinduism; a portion of the *Mahābhārata*, in which Lord Krishna instructs his disciple Arjuna on the nature of God, the universe, and the supreme Self, and on the different forms of yoga, the nature of dharma, and the way to attain liberation.

Bhagawan [*bhagavan*]
(*lit.*, the Lord) One endowed with the six attributes or powers of infinity: spiritual power, righteousness, glory, splendor, knowledge, and renunciation. A term of great honor. Swami Muktananda's Guru is known as Bhagawan Nityananda. *See also* Nityananda, Bhagawan.

Bhakta(s) [*bhakta*]
A devotee, a lover of God; a follower of *bhakti* yoga, the path of love and devotion.

Bhakti (Yoga) [*bhakti*]
The path of devotion described by the sage Narada in his *Bhakti Sūtras*; a path to union with the Divine based on the continual offering of love and constant remembrance of the Lord.

Bhakti Sutras [*bhaktisūtra*]
The classic scripture on devotion composed by the sage Narada, also known as the Philosophy of Love. *See also* Bhakti (Yoga).

Bhavartha Ramayana
[*bhavārtha rāmāyaṇa*]
A sixteenth-century rendition of Valmiki's *Rāmāyana*, composed in the Marathi language by Eknath Maharaj.

Birbal
A brilliant wit and poet, and the friend and minister of King Akbar.

Blue Being
The form that exists within the Blue Pearl; the Lord who grants the final vision.

Blue Pearl [*nīla bindu*]
Also referred to as Neeleshwari, the Blue Goddess; a brilliant blue light, the size of a tiny seed; the subtle abode of the inner Self and the vehicle by means of which the soul travels from one world to another either in meditation or at the time of death. Swami Muktananda writes extensively about his powerful inner visions of the Blue Pearl in his spiritual autobiography, *Play of Consciousness*.

Brahma [*brahmā*]
The Absolute Reality manifested as the active Creator of the universe, who is personified as one of the three gods of the Hindu trinity. The other two are Vishnu, who represents the principle of sustenance, and Shiva, who represents the principle of destruction.

Brahmamuhurta [*brahmamūhurta*]
The period of time between 3:00 A.M. and 6:00 A.M., described in the scriptures as the best time for meditation and worship.

Brahman [*brahman*]
The Absolute Reality or all-pervasive supreme Principle of the universe. The nature of Brahman is described in the Upanishads and in Vedantic philosophy as: *sat* (Existence absolute), *chit* (Consciousness absolute), and *ānanda* (Bliss absolute). *See also* Sat Chit Ananda.

Brahmananda [*brahmānanda*]
(19th century) Rajasthani saint who lived in Pushkar, where he was a devout worshiper at the only temple in India dedicated to Brahma. A great poet and yogi, he wrote *Ishwara Darshan* ("the vision of God") proclaiming that "God is manifest." He also expressed his learning and wisdom in the form of ecstatic *bhajans*.

Causal Body
One of the supraphysical bodies; the state of deep sleep occurs here. This body is black in color and the size of a fingertip.

Chakra(s) [*cakra*]
(*lit.*, wheel) A center of energy located in the subtle body where the *nāḍīs* converge, giving the appearance of a lotus. Six major *chakras* lie within the *sushumnā nāḍī*, or central channel. They are: *mūlādhāra*, at the base of the spine; *svādhishthāna*, at the root of the reproductive organs; *manipura*, at the navel; *anāhata*, the "lotus of the heart"; *vishuddha*, at the throat; and *ājñā* between the eyebrows. When it is awakened, the Kundalini flows upward from the *mūlādhāra* to the seventh *chakra*, the *sahasrāra*, at the crown of the head. *See also* Kundalini; Shaktipat.

Chapati [*capāti*]
Unleavened Indian bread that resembles a thin pancake.

Chiti Shakti [*citiśakti*]
The power of universal Consciousness; the creative aspect of God portrayed as the universal Mother, the Goddess, who is known by many names.

Dal [*dāla*]
Split legumes of many varieties used as a staple in Indian cooking. They are of five types: masoor dal, red lentil, mung dal, yellow and green split peas.

Darshan [*darśana*]
(*lit.*, to have sight of; viewing) 1) A glimpse or vision of a saint; being in

the presence of a holy being; seeing God or an image of God. 2) The monthly magazine of Siddha Yoga.

Datta, Dattatreya [*dattatreya*]
A divine incarnation known as the lord of *avadhūts* and often revered as the embodiment of the supreme Guru.

Devi [*devī*]
(*lit.*, resplendent) The great Mother Goddess; the beloved of Shiva who represents Shakti or cosmic energy. In Her benign form, the *devī* is known as Parvati. In Her fierce aspect, She is known as Kali and Durga.

Dharma [*dharma*]
(*lit.*, what holds together) Essential duty; the law of righteousness; living in accordance with the divine will. The highest dharma is to recognize the Truth in one's own heart.

Dhoti(s) [*dhoti*]
Traditional dress for men in India; a length of cloth wrapped around the waist.

Dhyana [*dhyāna*]
Meditation; the seventh stage of yoga described by Patanjali in the *Yoga Sūtras*. *See also* Ashtanga Yoga.

Diksha [*dīkṣā*]
Any religious initiation; initiation given by a Guru usually by imparting a mantra; in Siddha Yoga, the spiritual awakening of the disciple by Shaktipat. *See also* Siddha Yoga; Shaktipat.

Eight Psychic Powers
See Siddhi(s).

Eknath Maharaj
[*ekanātha mahārāja*]
(1528-1609 A.D.) A householder poet-saint of Maharashtra. The author of several hundred *abhangas*, or devotional poems, he was expelled from the brahmin caste because of his attempts to banish untouchability. By writing on religious subjects in the vernacular, Eknath ushered in a spiritual revival

among the people.

Five Elements
Ether, air, fire, water, earth: these comprise the elemental basis of the universe.

Five Organs of Action
The powers of speaking, grasping, locomotion, procreation, and excretion.

Five Senses of Perception
Hearing, seeing, touching, tasting, and smelling.

Four Aspects of the Mind
Manas, which has the capacity to think; *chitta*, the subconscious mind; *ahamkāra*, the ego; and *buddhi*, which has the power to discriminate.

Four States
The states of waking, dream, deep sleep, and samadhi, which are experienced in the physical, subtle, causal, and supracausal bodies respectively. *See also* Blue Pearl; Turiya.

Ganeshpuri [*gaṇeśapurī*]
A village at the foot of Mandagni Mountain in Maharashtra, India. Bhagawan Nityananda settled in this region where yogis have performed spiritual practices for thousands of years. The ashram founded by Swami Muktananda at his Guru's command is built on this sacred land.

Gita [*gītā*]
See Bhagavad Gita, Guru Gita.

Gopi(s) [*gopī*]
The milkmaids of Vraja, childhood companions and devotees of Krishna. They are revered as the embodiments of the ideal states of ecstatic devotion to God. *See also* Krishna.

Guru, Guruji, Gurudev
[*guru, gurudeva*]
(*lit.*, *gu*, darkness; *ru*, light; *deva*, lord) A spiritual Master who has attained oneness with God and who is therefore able both to initiate seekers and to guide them on the spiritual path to liberation. A Guru is also required to

be learned in the scriptures and must belong to a lineage of Masters. *See also* Shaktipat; Siddha.

Gurubhava [*gurubhāva*]
(*lit.*, Guru, Master; *bhāva*, becoming; being) A feeling of absorption in or identification with the Guru.

Guru Gita [*gurugītā*]
(*lit.*, song of the Guru) An ancient, sacred text; a garland of mantras that describes the nature of the Guru, the Guru-disciple relationship, and meditation on the Guru. In Siddha Yoga Meditation ashrams, the *Guru Gītā* is chanted every morning.

Guru Om [*guru om*]
The mantra by which the inner Self is remembered in the form of the Guru.

Guruseva [*gurusevā*]
Selfless service; work offered to the Guru, performed with an attitude of nondoership and without attachment.

Hanuman [*hanumān*]
(*lit.*, heavy-jawed) A demigod in the form of a huge white monkey who is one of the heroes of the *Rāmāyana*. Hanuman's unparalleled strength was exceeded only by his perfect devotion to Lord Rama, for whom he performed many acts of bravery and daring.

Hari Giri Baba [*harigiri bābā*]
A Siddha from Vaijapur, Maharashtra, who bestowed great love and affection on Swami Muktananda.

Hatha Yoga [*hathayoga*]
This yoga derives its name from the Sanskrit *ha* (sun) and *tha* (moon); it involves the attainment of the samadhi state through the systematic balancing of the solar and lunar *prānas* that flow respectively through the *pingalā* and *idā nādīs* of the human body. By the diligent practice, under expert supervision, of physical exercises which include *āsanas* (postures), *mudrās* (seals), *bandhas* (locks), *kriyās* (cleansing practices), and *prānāyāma* (breath

control), the adept hatha yogi carefully manages to merge the *prānas* flowing through the *idā* and *pingalā* and cause them to flow into the central *nādī* (*sushumnā*) instead. When this energy rises to the *sahasrāra*, it brings the experience of Self-realization.

Hatha Yoga Pradipika
[*hathayogapradīpikā*]
An authoritative fifteenth-century treatise on hatha yoga written by Svatmarama Yogi, which describes the practice of various hatha yoga techniques, such as *prānāyāma*, *āsana*, *mudrā*, etc.

Heart Chakra
The twelve-petaled subtle energy center of the heart. *See also* Chakra(s).

Japa [*japa*]
(*lit.*, prayer uttered in a low voice) Repetition of a mantra, either silently or aloud. *See also* Mantra.

Jnana Yoga [*jñānayoga*]
The yoga of knowledge; a spiritual path based on continuous contemplation and self-inquiry.

Jnaneshwar Maharaj
[*jñāneśvara mahārāja*]
(1275-1296 A.D.) Foremost among the poet-saints of Maharashtra, India, he was born into a family of saints. His older brother, Nivrittinath, was his Guru. His younger brother, Sopan, and sister, Muktabai, also attained enlightenment in childhood. At the age of 21, Jnaneshwar took live samadhi (a yogi's voluntary departure from the body) in Alandi, where, to this day, his samadhi shrine continues to attract thousands of seekers.

Jnani [*jñāni*]
An enlightened being; a follower of the path of knowledge. *See also* Jnana Yoga.

Jyotirlinga(m) [*jyotirlinga(m)*]
(*lit.*, lingam of light) One of the twelve great *Shivalinga* of India. *See also* Linga(m).

Kabir [kabīra]

(1440-1518) A great poet-saint and mystic who lived his life as a simple weaver in Benares, India. His followers included both Hindus and Muslims, and his influence was a powerful force in overcoming the fierce religious factionalism of the day. Bracing and penetrating, ecstatic and sobering, his poems describe the experience of the Self, the greatness of the Guru, and the nature of true spirituality. They are still being studied and sung all over the world.

Kailas, Mount [kailāsa]

A mountain peak in the Tibetan region of the Himalayas revered as the abode of Lord Shiva and a sacred place of pilgrimage.

Karma [karma]

(lit., action) 1) Any action — physical, verbal, or mental; 2) destiny, which is caused by past actions, mainly those of previous lives. There are three categories of karma: that destined to be played out in the current lifetime; that for future lives, currently stored in seed form; and that created in the present lifetime. The first occurs even if the individual attains liberation in this lifetime; the other two are burned up when liberation is attained.

Kashi [kāśi]

The city of Varanasi, or Benares, sacred to Lord Shiva, located in North India on the banks of the river Ganges. According to Hindu tradition, whoever dies in this city attains liberation.

Krishna [kṛṣṇa]

(lit., the dark one; the one who attracts irresistibly) The eighth incarnation of Lord Vishnu. His life story is told in the *Shrīmad Bhāgavatam*; his spiritual teachings are contained in the *Bhagavad Gītā*, a portion of the epic *Mahābhārata*. *See also* Vishnu.

Kriya [kriyā]

A gross (physical) or subtle (mental, emotional) purificatory movement initiated by the awakened Kundalini. *Kriyās* purify the body and nervous system so as to allow a seeker to sustain the energy of higher states of consciousness.

Kumkum [kumkum]

(lit., red-red) A red powder used in worship; also worn as an auspicious mark between the eyebrows, in remembrance of the Guru.

Kundalini [kuṇḍalinī]

(lit., coiled one) The supreme power, primordial Shakti, or energy that lies coiled at the base of the spine in the *mūlādhāra chakra* of every human being. Through the descent of grace (Shaktipat), this extremely subtle force, also described as a goddess, is awakened and begins to purify the whole system. As She travels upward through the central channel (*sushumnā nāḍī*), She pierces the various subtle energy centers (*chakras*) until She finally reaches the *sahasrāra* at the crown of the head. There, the individual self merges into the supreme Self in the marriage of Shiva and Shakti, and the cycle of birth and death comes to an end. Kundalini is described, in the sacred texts that praise Her, as constantly watching for an opportunity to bestow Her grace on the seeker. *See also* Chakra(s); Shaktipat.

Ladu [ladū]

An Indian sweet in the shape of a ball.

Laya Yoga [layayoga]

Absorption of the mind into the Self; dissolution; the interiorization of consciousness.

Lila [līlā]

Divine play; all of creation is often explained in Indian scriptures as the *līlā*, or divine play, of God.

Linga(m) [liṅga(m)]

(lit., mark or characteristic) Shiva's sacred symbol representing his creative power; an oval-shaped emblem of Shiva made of stone, metal, or clay.

Lotus Feet
The lotus feet of the Guru are said to embody Shiva and Shakti, knowledge and action, the emission and reabsorption of creation. They are a mystical source of grace and illumination, and a figurative term for the Guru's teachings.

Madhavacharya [*mādhavācārya*]
(thirteenth century) The founder of the doctrine of dualism (*dvaita*) based on the *Vedānta Sūtras*.

Maha [*mahā*]
A prefix meaning great.

Mahabharata [*mahābhārata*]
An epic poem in Sanskrit, composed by the sage Vyasa, which recounts the struggle between the Kaurava and Pandava brothers over the disputed kingdom of Bharat. Within this vast narrative is contained a wealth of Indian secular and religious lore. The *Bhagavad Gītā* occurs in the latter portion of the *Mahābhārata*.

Maharaj [*mahārāja*]
(*lit.*, great king) A title of great respect for a saint or holy person.

Mahasamadhi [*mahāsamādhi*]
(*lit.*, the great union) 1) A realized yogi's conscious departure from the physical body at death. 2) A celebration on the anniversary of a great being's departure from the physical body. 3) A shrine erected at the place where a yogi has taken *mahāsamādhi*.

Mahatma(s) [*mahātma*]
(*lit.*, great soul) A title, meaning a great being or a great soul.

Maha Yoga [*mahāyoga*]
(*lit.*, the great yoga) *See* Siddha Yoga.

Mandukya Upanishad
[*māṇḍūkya upaniṣad*]
A portion of the *Atharva Veda* containing twelve verses on the syllable *Aum*. *See also* Om.

Mansur Mastana
(852-922) An ecstatic Sufi poet-saint who lived most of his life in Baghdad. He also journeyed through Iraq, Persia, India, and Kashmir to the periphery of China. He was hanged as a heretic for his pronouncement: *ana'l-Haqq*, "I am God," which orthodox Muslims of those days would not tolerate.

Mantra [*mantra*]
(*lit.*, sacred invocation; that which protects) The names of God; sacred words or divine sounds invested with the power to protect, purify, and transform the individual who repeats them.

Mantra Yoga [*mantra yoga*]
The yoga of the divine word; the science of sound. The path to union through mantra yoga is based on repetition of the name(s) of God and contemplation of their meaning.

Maya [*māyā*]
(*lit.*, to measure) The term used in Vedanta for the power that veils the true nature of the Self and projects the experiences of multiplicity and separation from God. The force of maya conceals the ultimate Truth, creating the illusion that the real is unreal, the unreal is real, and the temporary is everlasting.

Meru, Mount [*meru*]
A mountain in the Himalayas, considered in ancient India to be the center of the earth.

Mira, Mirabai [*mīrā, mīrābāī*]
(1433-1468) A Rajasthani queen famous for her poems of devotion to Lord Krishna. She was so absorbed in love for Krishna that when she was given poison by vindictive relatives, Mirabai drank it as nectar and remained unharmed.

Muladhara [*mūlādhāra*]
The first *chakra*, or lowest of the seven major energy centers in the subtle body, situated at the base of the spine, where consciousness deals mainly with survival. Here the Kundalini lies

coiled three and a half times, dormant until awakened by grace. *See also* Chakra(s), Kundalini, Shaktipat.

Mundaka Upanishad
[*muṇḍaka upaniṣad*]
This Upanishad speaks of the knowledge of Brahman and the need for a Guru, and also describes rebirth and liberation. *See also* Upanishad(s).

Nada [*nāda*]
(*lit.*, sound) Inner sounds heard during advanced stages of meditation; celestial harmonies; the spontaneous unstruck sound experienced in the *sushumnā nāḍī.*

Narada [*nārada*]
A divine *rishi*, or seer, who was a great devotee and servant of Lord Vishnu. He appears in many of the Puranas and is the author of the *Bhakti Sūtras*, the authoritative text on devotion. *See also* Bhakti (Yoga).

Nirguna [*nirguṇa*]
(*lit.*, without a quality) The aspect of God without form or attributes. *See also* Saguna.

Nirvana [*nirvaṇa*]
Spiritual liberation.

Nirvikalpa Samadhi
[*nirvikalpa samādhi*]
(*lit.*, samadhi without form) The highest state of meditative union with the Absolute that is beyond attribute, thought, or image.

Nityananda, Bhagawan
[*nityānanda bhagavān*]
(d. 1961; *lit.*, the lord of eternal bliss) Also known as Bade Baba (Elder Baba). Very little is known of Bhagawan Nityananda's early life; he was a born Siddha, living his entire life in the highest state of consciousness. He was seen first in south India and later traveled to Maharashtra, where the village of Ganeshpuri grew up around him. He spoke very little, yet thousands of people would queue for hours for a glimpse of him and to experience the profound blessing of his presence. His Samadhi Shrine is located at the site of his original quarters in Ganeshpuri, about a mile from Gurudev Siddha Peeth, the principal ashram of Siddha Yoga Meditation. In both Gurudev Siddha Peeth and Shree Muktananda Ashram in South Fallsburg, New York, Swami Muktananda has dedicated a temple of meditation to honor Bhagawan Nityananda's *mūrti*, or statue.

Niyama(s) [*niyama*]
Daily observances recommended for the practice of yoga such as cleanliness, contentment, and mental and physical discipline. *See also* Yama(s).

Om [*om*]
The primal sound from which the universe emanates. Also written *Aum*, it is the inner essence of all mantras.

Omkara [*omkāra*]
See Om.

Om Namah Shivaya
[*om namah śivāya*]
(*lit.*, Om, I bow to Shiva) The Sanskrit mantra of the Siddha Yoga lineage is known as the great redeeming mantra because of its power to grant both worldly fulfillment and spiritual realization. *Om* is the primordial sound; Shiva denotes divine Consciousness, the Lord who dwells in every heart.

Parashurama [*paraśurāma*]
A great being who taught the art of war to Dronacharya and Bhishma in the epic *Mahābhārata. See also* Mahabharata.

Patanjali [*patañjali*]
A fourth-century sage and author of the famous *Yoga Sūtras*, the exposition of one of the six orthodox philosophies of India and the authoritative text of the path of *rāja yoga. See also* Ashtanga Yoga; Yoga Sutras.

Prana [*prāṇa*]
The vital life-sustaining force of both the body and the universe. To carry out

its work, *prana* pervades the body in five forms: *prāna*, inhalation, the primary support of the heart; *apāna*, exhalation, the power that works downward to expel waste matter; *samāna*, the power that distributes the nourishment from food to all parts of the body; *vyāna*, the power of movement within the seventy-two million *nādīs*, or nerve channels of the subtle body; and *udāna*, the power that carries energy upward, giving strength and radiance to the body.

Pranayama [*prāṇāyāma*]
The yogic science through which the *prana* or vital force is brought under control and stabilized, a necessary condition in the instigation of the Self-realization process. In hatha yoga, *prānāyāma* is achieved through specific breathing exercises, since there is a link between the physical breath and the subtle *prāna*. In Siddha Yoga, *prānāyāma* occurs spontaneously through the inner workings of the awakened Kundalini and is often attended by automatic changes in the breathing pattern.

Prasad [*prasāda*]
A blessed or divine gift; often refers to food that has first been offered to God and later distributed.

Pratyabhijnahridayam
[*pratyabhijñāhrdayam*]
(*lit.*, the heart of the doctrine of recognition) An eleventh-century treatise by Kshemaraj that summarizes the *pratyabhijñā* philosophy of Kashmir Shaivism. It states, in essence, that individuals have forgotten their true nature by identifying with the body and that realization is a process of recognizing or remembering one's true nature (*pratyabhijñā*), which is the inner Self of supreme bliss and love.

Prayag Kumbha Mela
[*prayāga kumbha mela*]
A spiritual festival held every twelve years that attracts hundreds of thousands of devotees from all over India. Prayag, a holy place of pilgrimage, is at the confluence of three sacred rivers of India: the Ganges, the Yamuna, and the Saraswati.

Prema [*prema*]
Divine love. *See also* Bhakti (Yoga).

Puja [*pūjā*]
Worship. 1) The performance of worship. 2) An altar with images of the Guru or deity and objects used in worship.

Punyatithi [*punyātithi*]
The anniversary of a great being's death.

Purana(s) [*purāṇa*]
(*lit.*, ancient legends) The eighteen sacred books by the sage Vyasa containing stories, legends, and hymns about the creation of the universe, the incarnations of God, the teachings of various deities, and the spiritual legacies of ancient sages and kings.

Purusha [*puruṣa*]
The limited individual soul.

Radha [*rādhā*]
The childhood companion and beloved of Krishna who is celebrated in Indian tradition as the embodiment of devotion to God.

Raja Yoga [*rājayoga*]
The discipline of quieting the mind according to Patanjali's *Yoga Sūtras*. It includes concentration, meditation, and samadhi. *See also* Ashtanga Yoga.

Rajas [*rajas*]
One of the three essential qualities (*gunas*) of nature that determine the inherent characteristics of all created things. *Rajas* is associated with activity and passion.

Ram, Rama [*rāma*]
(*lit.*, pleasing; delight) The seventh incarnation of Lord Vishnu, Rama is seen as the embodiment of dharma and is the object of great devotion. He is the central character in the Indian epic *Rāmāyana*. *See also* Ramayana.

Ramakrishna Paramahamsa
[rāmakṛṣṇa paramahaṃsa]
(1836-1886) A great saint of Bengal;
the Guru of Swami Vivekananda and
the founder of the Ramakrishna Order
of monks.

Ramayana [rāmāyaṇa]
Attributed to the sage Valmiki and one
of the great epic poems of India, the
Rāmāyaṇa recounts the life and
exploits of Lord Rama, the seventh
incarnation of Vishnu. Rama, once the
king of Ayodhya, is forced into exile in
the forest with his wife, Sita (a form of
Lakshmi), and his brother Lakshmana.
Later Sita is captured by the demon-
king Ravana and taken to Sri Lanka.
She is rescued by Rama, with the help
of Hanuman, chief of the monkeys and
an embodiment of devotion and service
to the Lord. The story, rich with characters, subplots, and spiritual meaning,
has been told and retold through the
ages by saints, poets, scholars, and
common folk.

Rang Avadhut [rāṇga avadhūta]
A twentieth-century Siddha whom
Baba Muktananda met during his trav-
els through India.

Rasa [rasa]
Nectar, flavor; a subtle energy of rich-
ness, sweetness, and delight.

Riddhi(s) [ṛddhi]
Supernatural powers.

Rig Veda [ṛgveda]
One of the four Vedas, the *Rig Veda* is
composed of over one thousand hymns
of wisdom and contains some of the
world's greatest poetry. This Veda is
intended for the priest whose function it
is to recite the hymns inviting the gods
to the fire rituals. *See also* Veda(s).

Rudram [rudram]
A chant to Rudra from the *Krishna
Yajur Veda* in which the Lord in His
many manifestations is offered repeated
salutations. *See also* Veda(s).

Sadguru [sadguru]
A true Guru; divine Master. *See also*
Guru.

Sadgurunath Maharaj ki Jay!
[sadgurunātha mahārāja kī jaya]
("I hail the Master who has revealed
the Truth to me") An exalted, joyful
expression of gratitude to the Guru for
all that has been received.

Sadhana [sādhana]
A spiritual discipline or path; practices,
both physical and mental, on the spiritual path.

Sadhu [sādhu]
A wandering monk or ascetic; a holy
being; a practitioner of sadhana.

Saguna [saguṇa]
Having attributes; the personal aspect
of God. *See also* Nirguna.

Sahasrara [sahasrāra]
The thousand-petaled *chakra*, or spiritual energy center, at the crown of
the head, where one experiences the
highest states of consciousness. It is
the seat of Lord Shiva, the supreme
Guru. When the Kundalini Shakti
unites with Shiva in the *sahasrāra*, the
meditator achieves the state of enlightenment, or Self-realization. *See also*
Chakra(s); Kundalini.

Sai Baba of Shirdi
(1838-1918) One of the great Siddhas of
modern times. His samadhi shrine at
Shirdi is a popular place of pilgrimage.

Samadhi [samādhi]
A transcendental state of awareness in
which one experiences the Supreme
Reality and becomes Self-realized. This
state occurs when the topmost *chakra*,
the *sahasrāra*, is activated. There are
different types of samadhi depending
upon the degree of activation and the
type of yoga employed. In Siddha Yoga,
the samadhi state is not attended by
unconsciousness to the external world;
rather, one experiences *sahaja* (natural)
samadhi, in which one remains fully

alert and perceives the all-pervasiveness of universal Consciousness throughout daily activities.

Samadhi Shrine [*samādhi*]
After their *mahāsamādhi* (*lit.*, the great samadhi or final union of the individual consciousness with the Absolute), great yogis and saints are buried seated in a yogic posture and surrounded with precious and sacred objects. Pervaded by the rays of divine love and wisdom, the saints' resting places are tended with the utmost reverence as centers of prayer and meditation, and a source of blessings for all who come there.

Samsara [*saṃsāra*]
The world of change, mutability, and death; the world of becoming.

Samvat [*saṃvat*]
A year; in the year of.

Sannyasa [*saṃnyāsa*]
1) Monkhood. 2) The ceremony and vows in which one renounces the responsibilities and privileges of worldly life and dedicates oneself exclusively to the goal of Self-realization and service to God. 3) In India, traditionally, the final stage of life, which occurs after all worldly obligations have been fulfilled.

Sat Chit Ananda [*sat cit ānanda*]
The nature of the Supreme Reality. *Sat* is Being, that which exists in all times, in all places, and in all things; *chit* is Consciousness, that which illumines all things; and *ānanda* is supreme Bliss.

Satsang [*satsaṅga*]
(*lit.*, the company of the Truth) The company of saints and devotees; a gathering of devotees for the purpose of chanting, meditation, and listening to scriptural teachings or readings.

Self
The Atman, or divine Consciousness residing in the individual, described as the witness of the mind or the pure I-awareness.

Shaivagama [*śaivāgama*]
A collection of texts expounding the Shaiva philosophy. It consists of ten dualistic Shastras, eighteen Shastras that teach identity in difference, and sixty-four nondualistic Shastras expounded by Shiva.

Shaivatantra [*śaivatantra*]
Those portions of the *shaivāgama* that deal with yoga, initiation, ritual, mantra, and mystical diagrams (*yantras*), gestures (*mudrās*], and postures (*āsanas*). The *Vijñāna Bhairava* is part of the *shaivatantra*.

Shakti [*śakti*]
Force, energy; spiritual power; according to Shaivite philosophy, the divine or cosmic energy that manifests the universe; the dynamic aspect of supreme Shiva. *See also* Chiti Shakti; Kundalini.

Shaktipat [*śaktipāta*]
(*lit.*, descent of grace) A yogic initiation in which the Siddha Guru transmits his spiritual energy into the aspirant, thereby awakening the aspirant's dormant Kundalini. There are four different ways in which Shaktipat can be received: *sparsha dīkshā*, through the Guru's physical touch; *mantra dīkshā*, through his words; *drik dīkshā*, through his look; and *manasa dīkshā*, through his thoughts. *See also* Guru; Kundalini.

Shambhavi Mudra
[*śāmbhavī mudrā*]
(*lit.*, state of supreme Shiva) A state of spontaneous or effortless samadhi in which the eyes become focused within, not seeing any outer objects. Breathing is suspended without any effort and the mind delights in the inner Self without any attempt at concentration.

Shiva [*śiva*]
1) A name for the all-pervasive Supreme Reality. As the deity and highest Principle of the Shaivite tradition, Shiva performs the five cosmic functions of creation, maintenance, dissolution, concealment, and grace-

bestowal. 2) One of the Hindu trinity of gods, representing God as the destroyer; in his personal form, he is portrayed as a yogi wearing a tiger skin and holding a trident, snakes coiling around his neck and arms. He is attended by a host of goblins, ghosts, and demons. Paradoxically, he is also *karunābde*, "the ocean of compassion," and *ashutosha*, "he who is easily pleased." He is also portrayed in sweet family portraits with his beloved, Parvati, and their son Ganesh. His dialogues with Parvati, in which he is the supreme Guru and she takes the part of the disciple to ask for knowledge of liberation, give rise to such sacred texts as *Shree Guru Gītā*, recited daily in Siddha Yoga Meditation ashrams.

Shivalinga(m) [*śivalinga(m)*]
(*lit.*, mark or characteristic) Shiva's sacred symbol representing His creative power; an oval-shaped emblem of Lord Shiva made of stone, metal, or clay.

Shivaratri [*śivarātri*]
(*lit.*, night of Shiva) The night of the new moon in late February that is especially sacred to Lord Shiva. Devotees repeat the mantra *Om Namah Shivāya* throughout the night; on this night, each repetition is said to equal the merit of a thousand repetitions.

Shiva Sutras [*śivasūtra*]
A Sanskrit text revealed by Lord Shiva to the ninth-century sage Vasuguptacharya. It consists of seventy-seven sutras or aphorisms, which according to tradition were found inscribed on a rock in Kashmir. The *Shiva Sūtras* are the scriptural authority for the philosophical school known as Kashmir Shaivism.

Shravan [*śrāvana*]
The month of the Indian calendar that corresponds to July-August.

Shree [*śrī*]
A term of respect that means "wealth, prosperity, glory, and success" and

signifies mastery of all these.

Shree Gurudev Ashram
[*śri gurudeva aśrama*]
Former name of Gurudev Siddha Peeth, the ashram of Swami Muktananda Paramahamsa in Ganeshpuri, near Bombay, India.

Shrimad Bhagavatam
[*śrīmad bhāgavatam*]
One of the Puranas, it consists of ancient legends of the various incarnations of the Lord, including the life and exploits of Lord Krishna and stories of the sages and their disciples.

Shukadev [*śukadeva*]
(dates unknown) A great sage of ancient times, the son of Vyasa and a disciple of King Janaka. He is mentioned in many scriptures, but is most famous as the narrator of the *Shrīmad Bhāgavatam*. *See also* Shrimad Bhagavatam.

Siddha [*siddha*]
A perfected yogi; one who is in the state of unity-consciousness and who has achieved mastery over the senses and their objects; one whose experience of the supreme Self is uninterrupted and whose identification with the ego has been dissolved.

Siddha Guru [*siddha guru*]
One who has attained the state of enlightenment and who has the capacity to awaken the dormant spiritual energy of a disciple and guide him or her to the state of the Truth. *See also* Sadguru.

Siddhaloka [*siddhaloka*]
(*lit.*, world of the perfected beings) A world of blue light, in which the great Siddha Masters dwell in perpetual bliss; described by Swami Muktananda in his spiritual autobiography, *Play of Consciousness.*

Siddha Yoga [*siddhayoga*]
(*lit.*, the yoga of perfection) A path to union of the individual and the Divine that begins with Shaktipat, the inner

awakening by the grace of a Siddha Guru. Swami Chidvilasananda, Swami Muktananda's chosen successor, is the living Master of this path. Siddha Yoga is known as *mahāyoga* because Shaktipat initiation sets in motion a spontaneous and intelligent process in which any form of yoga will occur within the seeker according to need and temperament. *See also* Guru; Kundalini; Shaktipat.

Siddhi(s) [*siddhi*]
Supernatural powers that may be attained through yogic practices. The eight major *siddhis* are *animā*, the power of becoming as small as an atom; *mahimā*, the power to expand to any size; *laghimā*, the power to levitate, to become light; *garimā*, the power to become heavy; *prākāmya*, the power of seeing one's wishes fulfilled; *ishatva*, the power of lordship over everything; *vashitva*, the power to attract and control; and *yatrakāmā-vasāyitva*, infallibility of purpose.

Sita [*sītā*]
(*lit.*, the daughter of the earth) An embodiment of Lakshmi and the beloved of Lord Rama, the seventh incarnation of Lord Vishnu. Her story is told in the epic *Rāmāyana*.

Smriti(s) [*smṛti*]
Writings based on that which is remembered, not revealed; a body of literature produced by human authors.

So'ham/Hamsa [*so'ham/hamsa*]
(*lit.*, I am That) *So'ham* and *Hamsa* are identical mantras that describe the natural vibration of the Self, which occurs spontaneously with each incoming and outgoing breath. The breath is drawn in with the sound *ham* and goes out with the sound *so*. This process is described in detail by Swami Muktananda in his book *I Am That*. By becoming aware of *Hamsa*, a seeker experiences the identity between the individual self and the

supreme Self.

Subtle Body
The second of four bodies within a human being (the physical, subtle, causal, and supracausal bodies), experienced in the dream state. The *nādīs* and *chakras* are situated in the subtle body. *See also* Chakra(s); Supracausal Body.

Sundardas [*sundaradāsa*]
(1596-1689) A renowned poet-saint born in Rajasthan. The main collection of his *bhajans* in Hindi is the *Sundar Granthavāti*.

Supracausal Body
The fourth of the supraphysical bodies. The state of samadhi is experienced here. This body is blue and the size of a tiny seed.

Sushumna Nadi [*suṣumnā nādī*]
The central and most important of all the seventy-two million subtle nerve channels in the human body, the *sushumnā* extends from the *mūlādhāra chakra* at the base of the spine to the *sahasrāra*, or crown *chakra*, and contains all the other *chakras*, or subtle energy centers. When the *prāna*, or vital force, constantly flows through it, one becomes enlightened. *See also* Chakra(s).

Swami or Swamiji [*svāmi*]
A respectful term of address for a *sannyāsi* or monk.

Tandra [*tandrā*]
The state of higher consciousness between sleeping and waking that is experienced in meditation.

Tapasya [*tapasya*]
(*lit.*, heat) 1) Austerities. 2) The experience of heat that occurs during the process of practicing yoga. This heat is generated by friction between the mind and the heart, between the demands of the senses and the yearning for renunciation. It is said that this heat, "the fire of yoga," burns up all the impurities that lie between the seeker and the

experience of the Truth.

Tukaram Maharaj
[*tukarāma mahāraja*]
(1608-1650) A great poet-saint of Maharashtra born at Dehu, who received initiation in a dream. He wrote thousands of *abhangas* (devotional songs), many of which describe his sadhana and spiritual experiences, his initiation, his realization, and the glory of the divine Name.

Tulsi [*tulasī*]
An Indian herb, a species of basil, that is used in the worship of Lord Vishnu. It has great medicinal virtues.

Tulsidas [*tulasīdāsa*]
(1532-1623) The poet-saint of north India who wrote in Hindi the *Rāma Charitamānasa*, the life-story of Rama, still one of the most popular scriptures in India today.

Turiya [*turīya*]
The fourth or transcendental state, beyond the waking, dream, and deep-sleep states, in which the true nature of reality is directly perceived; the state of samadhi or deep meditation.

Turiyatita [*turīyātita*]
The state beyond *turīya*; the supremely blissful state of complete freedom from all duality and the awareness of the one Self in all; the final attainment of Siddha Yoga.

Upanishad(s) [*upaniṣad*]
(*lit.*, sitting close to; secret teachings) The inspired teachings, visions, and mystical experiences of the ancient sages, *rishis*, of India. These scriptures, exceeding one hundred texts, constitute "the end" or "final understanding" (*anta*) of the Vedas; hence the term Vedanta. With immense variety of form and style, all of these texts give the same essential teaching: that the individual soul and God are one.

Vajreshwari [*vajreśvarī*]
A village near Ganeshpuri in which

Swami Muktananda did his sadhana in a hut in the courtyard of an ancient temple dedicated to the Goddess.

Vasishtha [*vasiṣṭha*]
The legendary sage and Guru of Lord Rama, who epitomized the force of spiritual knowledge. He is the central figure of the *Yoga Vasishtha*, which is one of the most rigorous scriptures on the nature of the mind and the way to free it from illusion.

Veda(s) [*veda*]
(*lit.*, knowledge) Among the most ancient, revered, and sacred of the world's scriptures, the four Vedas are regarded as divinely revealed, eternal wisdom. They are the *Rig Veda, Atharva Veda, Sāma Veda,* and *Yajur Veda*.

Vedanta [*vedānta*]
(*lit.*, end of the Vedas) One of the six orthodox schools of Indian philosophy; the philosophy of absolute nondualism. *See also* Upanishad(s); Veda(s).

Vedantin(s) [*vedāntin*]
One who follows or expounds the philosophy of Vedanta.

Vedic
Of or pertaining to the Vedas.

Vimarshini, Shiva Sutra
Vimarshini [*śivasūtravimarśini*]
A tenth-century commentary on the *Shiva Sūtras*, one of three ancient commentaries still in existence and considered the most ancient and most learned. In the *Shiva Sūtra Vimarshini*, the sage Kshemaraj gives a lucid and detailed exposition of each *sūtra* (verse) in prose.

Vishnu [*viṣṇu*]
1) The all-pervasive Supreme Reality.
2) One of the Hindu trinity of gods, representing God as the sustainer of the universe; the deity of the Vaishnavas. In his personal form, he is portrayed as four-armed, holding a conch, a discus, a lotus, and a mace. He is dark blue in color. Vishnu incarnates in each *yuga* (cycle or world

period) to protect and save the world when the knowledge of dharma (truth and righteousness) is lost. Rama and Krishna are the best known of his incarnations (*avatārs*).

Viveka [*viveka*]
(*lit.*, discrimination; distinction) The faculty of discretion that enables a human being to distinguish between true and false, reality and illusion.

Yajna [*yajñā*]
1) A sacrificial fire ritual in which Vedic mantras are recited as different woods, fruits, grains, oils, yogurt, and ghee are poured into the fire as an offering to the Lord. 2) Any work or spiritual practice that is offered as worship to God.

Yama(s) [*yama*]
Restraints that are considered vital to one who is pursuing the yogic life, such as abstention from violence, falsehood, theft, and acquisitiveness. *See also* Ashtanga Yoga.

Yoga [*yoga*]
(*lit.*, union) The spiritual practices and disciplines that lead a seeker to evenness of mind, to the severing of the union with pain, and — through non-

doership — to skill in action. Ultimately, the path of yoga leads to the constant experience of the Self.

Yogashikha Upanishad
[*yogaśikha upaniṣad*]
One of the Yoga Upanishads that discusses the path of knowledge in all its aspects and expounds the subject of yoga as an aid to knowledge.

Yoga Sutras [*yogasūtra(s)*]
A collection of aphorisms, written in Sanskrit by Patanjali in the fourth century, which form the basic scripture of the path of *rāja* yoga. They expound different methods for the attainment of the state of yoga or samadhi, in which the movement of the mind ceases and the Witness of the mind rests in its own bliss. *See also* Patanjali.

Yogi, Yogini [*yogi, yoginī*]
One who practices yoga; also, one who has attained perfection through yogic practices. *See also* Yoga.

Zipruanna
A Siddha from Maharashtra whom Swami Muktananda dearly loved. It was Zipruanna who sent Baba to Bhagawan Nityananda.

FURTHER READING

SWAMI MUKTANANDA

Ashram Dharma

Play of Consciousness

From the Finite to the Infinite

Where Are You Going?

I Have Become Alive

The Perfect Relationship

Reflections of the Self

Secret of the Siddhas

I Am That

Kundalini

Mystery of the Mind

Does Death Really Exist?

Light on the Path

Lalleshwari

Mukteshwari

Meditate

Selected Essays

What Is an Intensive?

SWAMI CHIDVILASANANDA

Kindle My Heart

Inner Treasures

My Lord Loves a Pure Heart

Ashes at My Guru's Feet

Resonate with Stillness
(with Swami Muktananda)

You may learn more about the teachings and
practices of Siddha Yoga Meditation by contacting:

SYDA Foundation
371 Brickman Rd.
South Fallsburg, NY
12779-0600, USA
Tel: (914)434-2000

or

Gurudev Siddha Peeth
P.O. Ganeshpuri
PIN 401 206
District Thane
Maharashtra, India

For further information about books in print
by Swami Muktananda and Swami Chidvilasananda,
and editions in translation, please contact:

Siddha Yoga Meditation Bookstore
371 Brickman Rd.
South Fallsburg, NY
12779-0600, USA
Tel: (914) 434-0124